I0415911

June 2012

EMPLOYMENT FOR PEOPLE WITH DISABILITIES

Little Is Known about the Effectiveness of Fragmented and Overlapping Programs

G A O

Accountability ★ Integrity ★ Reliability

Highlights

Highlights of GAO-12-677, a report to congressional committees

June 2012

EMPLOYMENT FOR PEOPLE WITH DISABILITIES

Little Is Known about the Effectiveness of Fragmented and Overlapping Programs

Why GAO Did This Study

Many federal programs—within the Departments of Education, Labor, and Veterans Affairs; the Social Security Administration; and other agencies—help people with disabilities overcome barriers to employment. Section 21 of Pub. L. No. 111-139 requires GAO to identify and report annually on programs, agencies, offices, and initiatives that have duplicative goals or activities. GAO examined the extent to which programs that support employment for people with disabilities (1) provide similar services to similar populations and (2) measure effectiveness. GAO identified programs by searching the Catalog of Federal Domestic Assistance and consulting agency officials. GAO surveyed and interviewed agency officials to determine program objectives and activities. Nine agencies reviewed the draft report and five provided comments. Labor was concerned that GAO characterized its programs as fragmented and potentially duplicative. While multiple programs may be appropriate, GAO maintains that additional review and coordination may reduce inefficiencies and improve effectiveness among overlapping programs.

GAO is not recommending executive action at this time. In a recent report, GAO suggested the Office of Management and Budget (OMB) consider establishing governmentwide goals for employment of people with disabilities, and working with agencies that administer overlapping programs to determine whether consolidation might result in more effective and efficient delivery of services. GAO continues to believe these actions are needed and will follow up with OMB to determine their status.

View GAO-12-677. For more information, contact Daniel Bertoni at (202) 512-7215 or bertonid@gao.gov.

What GAO Found

GAO identified 45 programs that supported employment for people with disabilities in fiscal year 2010, reflecting a fragmented system of services. The programs were administered by nine federal agencies and overseen by even more congressional committees. All programs overlapped with at least one other program in that they provided one or more similar employment service to a similar population—people with disabilities. The greatest overlap occurred in programs serving veterans and servicemembers (19 programs) and youth and young adults (5 programs). In addition, GAO identified seven programs that did not limit eligibility to any particular population and were potentially available to veterans and servicemembers or youth. Some overlapping programs, such as those with specific eligibility requirements, have less potential for duplication—providing the same services to the same beneficiaries—than others. However, even when the potential for duplication of services is low, there may be inefficiencies associated with operating multiple programs that provide similar services to similar populations. Coordination across programs may help address fragmentation and potential duplication, but officials that GAO surveyed reported only limited coordination. However, among six selected programs that only serve people with disabilities—including the Department of Education's Vocational Rehabilitation program and the Social Security Administration's Ticket to Work program—officials cited more consistent coordination.

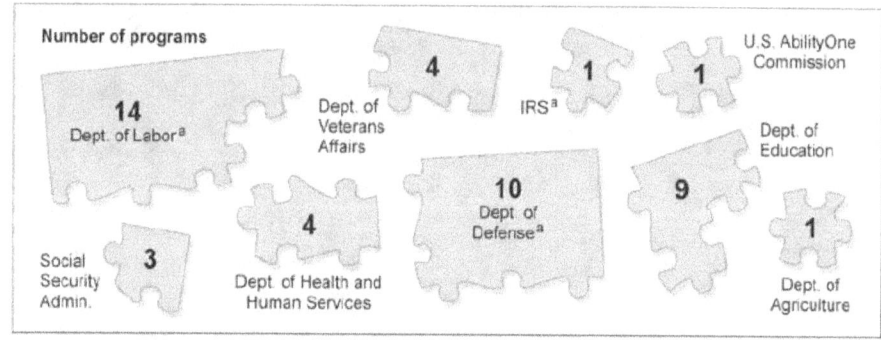

Number of programs

Source: GAO analysis.

[a]The Department of Labor jointly administers the Workforce Recruitment Program with the Department of Defense and the Work Opportunity Tax Credit with the Internal Revenue Service. These programs are therefore included under both the Department of Labor and the other administering agencies in the figure.

Most (32) of the 45 programs surveyed tracked at least one employment-related outcome measure for people with disabilities, but overall little is known about the effectiveness of these programs. The most commonly tracked outcomes for people with disabilities were "entered employment" (28 programs) and "employment retention" (18 programs). However, it may be difficult to compare outcomes across programs, in part, because of variation in the type and severity of participants' disabilities. In addition, only 10 of the 45 programs reported that an evaluation had been conducted in the last 5 years. Just one of the 45 programs (Job Corps) reported conducting an impact study—a study that would most clearly show whether the program (and not other factors) was responsible for improved employment outcomes for people with disabilities. However, additional studies are underway for at least two other programs.

_____ United States Government Accountability Office

Contents

Tables

Figures

Abbreviations

Education	Department of Education
GPRA	Government Performance and Results Act of 1993
GPRAMA	GPRA Modernization Act of 2010
Labor	Department of Labor
OMB	Office of Management and Budget
SSA	Social Security Administration
VA	Department of Veterans Affairs
VR	State Vocational Rehabilitation Services
VR agency	vocational rehabilitation agency
VR&E	Vocational Rehabilitation and Employment
WIA	Workforce Investment Act

United States Government Accountability Office
Washington, DC 20548

June 29, 2012

Congressional Committees

Nearly one in five people in the United States are reported to have a disability.[1] Although some people are born with disabilities, everyone is at risk of experiencing a short-term or long-term disability, whether through accidents, employment-related injuries and illnesses, disease, or aging. In addition, individuals may have mental disorders or developmental disabilities, which are severe chronic conditions resulting from mental and/or physical impairments that can begin at any time during development and last throughout a person's lifetime. A body of evidence indicates that many people with disabilities can and want to work. However, research has shown that people with disabilities may face multiple barriers to employment, including poor health or functioning; inadequate education, skills, or training; lack of transportation; lack of accessible workplaces or accommodations; and discrimination. Federal programs reported obligating more than $4 billion in fiscal year 2010 on employment-related supports for people with disabilities, compared to a significantly higher amount on income and medical supports for people with disabilities. Even with these expenditures, historically, people with disabilities have experienced higher unemployment and poverty rates than those without disabilities.

Over the years, many federal programs across a number of federal agencies have been created or have evolved to address barriers to employment for people with disabilities, resulting in a fragmented system of supports. Recently, we identified 50 programs administered by nine federal agencies that supported employment for people with disabilities.[2] This report provides additional information and context related to our work

---

[1] U.S. Census Bureau, Americans with Disabilities: 2005. (Washington, D.C.: December 2008). Data from the Survey of Income and Program Participation, June through September 2005.

[2] GAO, 2012 Annual Report: Opportunities to Reduce Duplication, Overlap, and Fragmentation, Achieve Savings, and Enhance Revenue, GAO-12-342SP (Washington, D.C.: Feb. 28, 2012). This report was our second annual report to Congress in response to the statutory requirement that we identify and report annually on federal programs, agencies, offices, and initiatives that have duplicative goals or activities, in accordance with Pub. L. No. 111-139, § 21, 124 Stat. 29 (2010), 31 U.S.C. § 712 Note.

GAO-12-677 Employment for People with Disabilities

and addresses the following objectives: (1) to what extent do federal programs that support employment for people with disabilities provide similar services to similar populations and (2) to what extent has the effectiveness of programs that support employment for people with disabilities been measured?

To address our first objective, we identified programs that support employment for people with disabilities by consulting with federal agency officials and researchers knowledgeable about employment and disability issues, searching the Catalog of Federal Domestic Assistance, and reviewing our previous work. Consistent with our prior work on duplication, we considered "programs" to include a variety of types of assistance—such as grants, initiatives, and tax expenditures—and will use that term throughout the report for simplicity. We included programs that served only people with disabilities, as well as programs that served a broader population but provided special consideration to people with disabilities or their employers.[3] We also included programs for wounded, ill, and injured servicemembers within our scope. After validating the list of programs with agency officials, we fielded a web-based survey to each program. The survey collected information on each program's objectives, eligibility requirements, services provided, outcome measures, and obligations, among other data. We incorporated data reliability checks into the survey instrument, reviewed documentation, and conducted follow-up interviews as necessary. We determined that the data used in this report were sufficiently reliable for the purposes of this report. We did not conduct an independent legal analysis to identify relevant programs or verify the program information provided by survey respondents. To further explore coordination efforts among overlapping programs, we selected six programs—administered by three different agencies—that serve only

---

[3]Specifically, in order to be considered within the scope of our work, agencies must have reported that their programs met at least one of the following criteria and provided an employment-related service in fiscal year 2010: (1) people with disabilities are mentioned in the legislation as a targeted group, (2) people are eligible for the program wholly because of a disability, (3) people are eligible for the program partially because of a disability, (4) people with disabilities are given special consideration in eligibility determinations, (5) people with disabilities are given priority in being served, or (6) employers of people with disabilities are a targeted group.

people with disabilities.[4] We conducted interviews with officials representing these six programs regarding their coordination efforts, challenges to coordination, and factors that facilitate or create barriers to coordination. To address our second objective, we collected data through our survey on program outcome measures and any studies or evaluations of program performance conducted since 2006. We reviewed the studies' methodologies to determine whether they met our definition of an impact study.[5] We conducted this performance audit from April 2011 to June 2012 in accordance with generally accepted government auditing standards. Those standards require that we plan and perform the audit to obtain sufficient, appropriate evidence to provide a reasonable basis for our findings and conclusions based on our audit objectives. We believe that the evidence obtained provides a reasonable basis for our findings and conclusions based on our audit objectives. See Appendix I for a more detailed description of our objectives, scope, and methodology.

Background

Improving and Modernizing Federal Disability Programs

In 2003, we first designated federal disability programs as a high-risk area because the programs require urgent attention and organizational transformation to ensure that they function in the most economical, efficient, and effective manner possible.[6] We have also reported that improving work participation among people with disabilities has been challenging in part because the United States has a patchwork of disability programs—developed individually over many years—and lacks

---

[4]The selected programs were the Department of Education's State Vocational Rehabilitation Services and Assistive Technology State Grant programs; the Department of Labor's Disability Employment Initiative; and the Social Security Administration's State Vocational Rehabilitation Cost Reimbursement, Work Incentives Planning and Assistance, and Ticket to Work programs. The Disability Employment Initiative was not included in our analysis of the 45 programs that support employment for people with disabilities because it is a new program, and it did not provide services in fiscal year 2010. We included this program in our analysis of program coordination because its purpose is to increase coordination across programs and agencies that support employment for people with disabilities.

[5]An impact study assesses the net effect of a program by comparing program outcomes with an estimate of what would have happened in the absence of the program.

[6]GAO, High-Risk Series: An Update, GAO-03-119 (Washington, D.C.: January 2003).

a unified set of national goals that guide coordination among programs or contribute to measuring desired outcomes.[7]

In February 2012, we identified programs administered by nine federal agencies that supported employment for people with disabilities, and many of these programs overlapped in that they provided similar services to similar populations.[8] We recommended that the Office of Management and Budget (OMB), in consultation with those agencies that administer programs that support employment for people with disabilities, take two actions to improve coordination and program effectiveness and efficiency: (1) consider establishing measurable, governmentwide goals for employment of people with disabilities, and (2) continue to work with executive agencies that administer overlapping programs to determine whether program consolidation might result in administrative savings and more effective and efficient delivery of services.

In response, the Office of Management and Budget (OMB) noted that, in fiscal year 2012, the administration's Domestic Policy Council will conduct an internal review of ways to improve the effectiveness of disability programs through better coordination and alignment of policies and strategies. OMB also noted that the administration has set governmentwide goals for employment and inclusion of people with disabilities in the federal government, among other ongoing and planned efforts to improve employment for people with disabilities.

GPRA Modernization Act of 2010

Responsibility for many federal efforts, including employment support for people with disabilities, lies with more than one agency, yet agencies face a range of challenges and barriers when they attempt to work collaboratively. Both Congress and the Executive Branch have recognized this, and in January 2011, the GPRA Modernization Act of 2010 (GPRAMA) was enacted, updating the Government Performance and Results Act of 1993.[9] GPRAMA establishes a new framework aimed at taking a more crosscutting and integrated approach for focusing on results and improving government performance. Effective implementation

---

[7]GAO, *Federal Disability Programs: More Strategic Coordination Could Help Overcome Challenges to Needed Transformation*, GAO-08-635 (Washington, D.C.: May 20, 2008).

[8]GAO-12-342SP.

[9]Pub. L. No. 111-352, 124 Stat. 3866 (2011); Pub. L. No. 103-62, 107 Stat. 285.

of the law could play an important role in clarifying desired outcomes, addressing program performance spanning multiple organizations, and facilitating future actions to reduce unnecessary duplication, overlap, and fragmentation.[10]

GPRAMA requires OMB to coordinate with agencies to establish outcome-oriented goals covering a limited number of crosscutting policy areas as well as goals to improve management across the federal government, and to develop a governmentwide performance plan for making progress toward achieving those goals. The performance plan is required to, among other things, identify the agencies and federal activities—including spending programs, tax expenditures, and regulations—that contribute to each goal, and establish performance indicators to measure overall progress toward these goals as well as the individual contribution of the underlying agencies and federal activities. GPRAMA also requires similar information at the agency level. Each agency is required to identify the various federal organizations and activities—both within and external to the agency—that contribute to its goals, and describe how the agency is working with other agencies to achieve its goals as well as any relevant crosscutting goals. OMB officials stated that their approach to responding to this requirement will address fragmentation among federal programs. OMB and the agencies within our scope identified several employment-related goals for fiscal year 2013, including a goal to increase the percentage of eligible servicemembers served by career readiness and preparedness programs, and a goal to provide 2 million workers with skills training by 2015 and improve the coordination and delivery of job training services. However, none of the governmentwide goals established for fiscal year 2013 relate specifically to employment for people with disabilities.

Members of Congress have expressed concern that there is no consolidated list of all federal government programs, and that individual federal agencies are not able to provide a list of all of their programs and initiatives. GPRAMA requires OMB to create a single website, no later than October 1, 2012, that lists each federal agency's programs. Agencies are required to identify how they define the term "program," consistent with guidance from OMB; a description of the purpose of each program and how it contributes to the mission and goals of the agency;

---

[10]GAO-12-342SP.

and information on funding for the current fiscal year and two previous fiscal years. In addition, in January 2012, OMB announced that it will work with agencies to identify a comprehensive list of programs, pursuant to the law. As a first step, OMB stated it will conduct a pilot for a selected group of agencies and bureaus with programs related to trade, exports, and competitiveness. Based on the pilot, OMB plans to issue guidance to all federal agencies detailing the approach to be taken to develop a governmentwide inventory of programs.

Fragmentation and Overlap Prevalent among 45 Programs Serving People with Disabilities

Fragmentation occurs when more than one federal agency (or organization within an agency) is involved in the same broad area of national need. As we have previously noted, fragmented programs that do not coordinate effectively could waste scarce funds, confuse and frustrate program beneficiaries, and limit the overall effectiveness of the federal effort.[11] We identified 45 programs that supported employment for people with disabilities in fiscal year 2010 and continued to do so as of April 2012.[12] (See app. III for a complete list of programs.) Oversight and administration of the programs is the responsibility of multiple congressional committees, executive agencies, and state and local offices. Most of the programs overlapped in that they provided similar services to similar populations; however, differences in specific eligibility criteria sometimes limited the potential for duplication. In general, coordination among the 45 programs was limited. Selected programs that serve only people with disabilities reported higher levels of coordination at the state and local levels.

---

[11]GAO-12-342SP.

[12]In our contribution to our governmentwide examination of duplication (GAO-12-342SP), we reported on 50 programs that supported employment for people with disabilities in fiscal year 2010. For this report, we have omitted six of these programs—two of which, that is, SSA's Mental Health Treatment Study and Youth Transition Demonstration, were demonstration studies of limited duration—that agency officials reported had been phased out or ended by April 2012, when we finalized our data (see app. II for details on the programs). In addition, we excluded an additional program—the Benefit Offset National Demonstration—because, while the program had obligations in fiscal year 2010, SSA officials reported that the demonstration did not begin enrolling participants until January 2011. In commenting on a draft of our prior report and, later, in verifying data previously provided, Department of Defense officials requested that we add three programs that they believed to be within the scope of this review. After reviewing the programs, we determined that two met our criteria and we included them in our analyses for this report. We did not include or review programs that may have been created or revised after fiscal year 2010.

Program Oversight and Administration Is Fragmented

Oversight and administration of programs that support employment for people with disabilities is fragmented among various congressional committees, multiple federal agencies, and state entities (see fig. 1). Agency officials reported that 27 of the 45 programs were created by statute, rather than at the agencies' initiative. At least 13 congressional committees are responsible for oversight of the 45 programs, which are administered by nine federal agencies. In some cases, a range of departments or offices within an agency are responsible for the programs. For example, several offices in the Department of Labor (Labor) administer 14 programs that provide employment-related services to people with disabilities. Further, the Department of Defense has 10 programs within its purview in part because each service branch administers its own program or programs to assist wounded, ill, and injured servicemembers with employment. Adding to the fragmented landscape, some of these federal programs are administered by governmental and nongovernmental state or local entities, either in collaboration or independently. In addition, agency officials noted that states have various governmental structures to administer the programs. For example, the Department of Education (Education) allocates formula funds to states to carry out the State Vocational Rehabilitation Services (VR) program. The state may create one vocational rehabilitation agency (VR agency) or designate a separate VR agency to serve individuals who are blind and a "general" agency for all other disability categories. In addition, each state may organize its VR agency or agencies within different government departments relative to other states, such as state departments of labor or education, or they may be free-standing agencies or commissions.

Figure 1: Multiple Congressional Committees, Federal and State Agencies, and Other Entities Oversee and Administer 45 Federal Programs that Support Employment for People with Disabilities

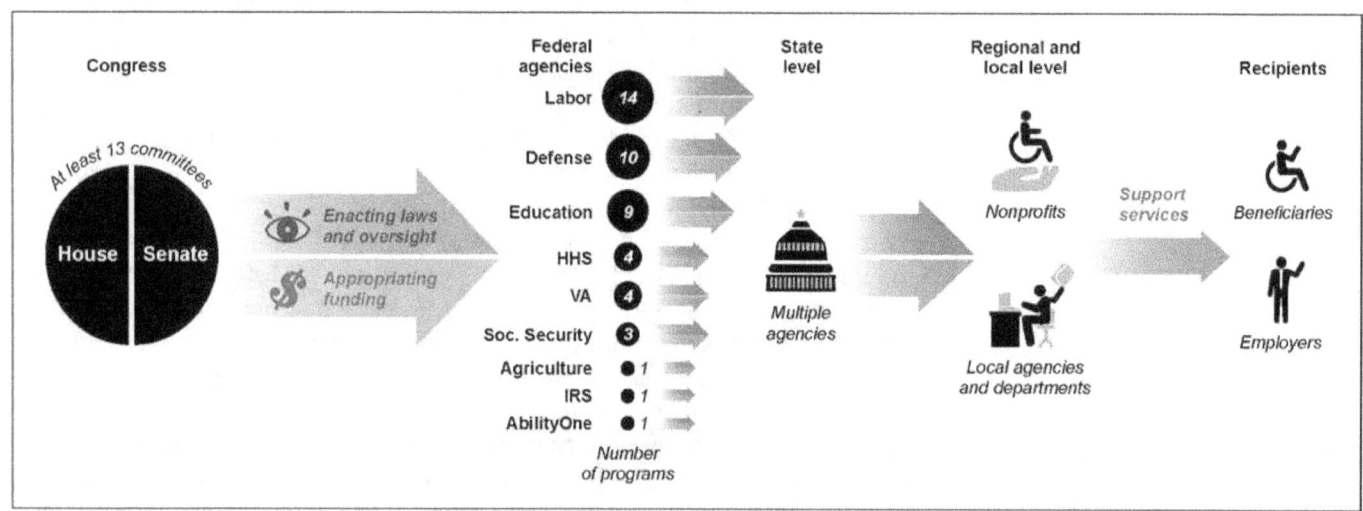

Source: GAO analysis of interviews with agencies and other relevant documentation.

Note: Labor jointly administers the Workforce Recruitment Program with the Department of Defense and the Work Opportunity Tax Credit with the Internal Revenue Service. These programs are therefore included under both Labor and the other administering agencies in the figure.

The specific definitions of disability and eligibility requirements that programs use—often established by law—vary, which may contribute to fragmentation. For example, officials from 34 programs collectively reported using at least 10 different definitions of disability, and 10 programs reported having no specific definition for disability. In addition, the 45 programs reported at least 26 specific limitations to eligibility, such as limiting services to Native Americans or people who are blind. The variation across programs allows policy makers and program officials to target certain populations and, as discussed later, may reduce the potential for duplicative services. However, variation in definitions of disability and eligibility requirements may lead to confusion among people with disabilities about their eligibility for a specific program, and may create additional administrative burdens for state and local agencies and private partners that deliver services.

To address fragmentation among programs that support employment for people with disabilities, at least two programs have been created to assist clients in determining what services and benefits they are eligible for, and which would best meet their needs. Specifically, according to agency officials, the Social Security Administration's (SSA) Work Incentives

Planning and Assistance program helps Social Security Disability Insurance beneficiaries and Supplemental Security Income disability recipients (for the purposes of this report, we will refer to these populations collectively as "SSA disability beneficiaries") understand SSA's complex work incentives and how working would affect their disability benefits or payments. In addition, agency officials noted that Labor's Disability Program Navigators, jointly funded with SSA, provided staff members in one-stop career centers to help people with disabilities navigate multiple employment programs and services to meet their employment needs.[13]

The number and range of programs makes it difficult to estimate the total federal funding dedicated to providing people with disabilities with employment supports or the number of individuals served. Programs we surveyed reported obligating about $4.1 billion to provide employment support to at least 1.5 million individuals with disabilities in fiscal year 2010, but these numbers may be largely underestimated for several reasons. (See table 1 for summary information on reported numbers of people served and obligations in fiscal year 2010; see app. III for detailed fiscal year 2010 participant and obligation data reported by each program.) Of the 23 programs serving only people with disabilities, 18 reported on the number of people with disabilities receiving employment supports and 18 reported data on obligations in fiscal year 2010. One program—Education's VR program—accounted for most of these funds and participants (the program obligated $3 billion to serve more than 1 million people with disabilities). Even less is known about expenditures on and the number of people receiving employment supports from the 22 programs serving people with and without disabilities. Specifically, only 13 of these programs reported how many people with disabilities received employment supports and 10 reported obligations spent on people with disabilities. Agency officials from some of these programs reported that they do not systematically collect information on whether participants have disabilities, while others indicated that program participants may not always disclose that they have a disability. SSA officials noted that Section 504 of the Rehabilitation Act of 1973, as amended—which prohibits federal agencies and programs that receive federal funding from

---

[13]The Disability Program Navigator program was not included in analyses for this report because it ended after fiscal year 2010. See appendix II. Best practices from the Disability Program Navigator, including this function, were incorporated into the Disability Employment Initiative, a new program.

GAO-12-677 Employment for People with Disabilities

discriminating against individuals with disabilities—limits programs' ability to require individuals to disclose that they have a disability. Other programs, such as Labor's Employer Assistance and Resource Network, serve employers of people with disabilities and do not track the number of people with disabilities who indirectly benefit from program services.

Table 1: Programs Reporting the Number of People with Disabilities Served and Obligations, Fiscal Year 2010

	Number of programs	Number of people with disabilities receiving employment support	Obligations for providing employment support to people with disabilities
Serve only people with disabilities or their families	23	1,313,046 (18 programs reporting)	$4.1 billion (18 programs reporting)
Serve people with and without disabilities	22	224,141 (13 programs reporting)	$7.3 million (10 programs reporting)
Total	**45**	**1,537,187**	**$4.1 billion**

Source: GAO analysis of survey data.

Overlap Was Greatest among Certain Programs

All 45 programs overlapped with at least one other program in that they provided one or more similar employment service to people with disabilities. To identify services provided, we asked survey respondents to indicate from a list of employment-related services and supports which ones their programs provide. Respondents indicated a range of services provided, with some services being provided more than others.[14] For example, survey responses revealed that 36 of the 45 programs provided employment counseling, assessment, and case management, with 23 providing these services to more than half of their participants. On the other hand, agency officials reported that 17 programs provided remedial academic English language skills and adult literacy assistance, with 4 of those providing it to more than half of their participants. Two programs reported providing tax expenditures related to workers with disabilities. For example, the Work Opportunity Tax Credit provides a tax credit to employers who hire individuals from target groups, including disabled veterans. In addition, two programs—Education's Randolph-Sheppard program and the U.S. AbilityOne Commission's AbilityOne Program—help create jobs for individuals with disabilities through the federal

---

[14]Survey respondents reported whether they provided the service to more than 50 percent of participants, less than 50 percent of participants, or that they provided the service but could not specify the level. We did not collect the number of participants receiving each service.

GAO-12-677 Employment for People with Disabilities

property management and procurement systems. Randolph-Sheppard licenses people who are blind to operate vending facilities on federal or other designated state properties. Under the AbilityOne program, federal government agencies are generally required to purchase certain goods and services from nonprofit agencies that employ people who are blind or have some other severe disability. Several programs also noted that they provided additional services not included on our list, such as financial supports, resume preparation, job coaching, transportation, and medical and psychiatric services.

Figure 2: Number of Programs Reporting Selected Employment Services Provided to People with Disabilities, Fiscal Year 2010

Service	More than 50%	Less than 50%	Extent unknown	Total
Employment-related information dissemination	18	10	10	38
Employment counseling, assessment, and case management	23	5	8	36
Job readiness skills	19	5	12	36
Job search or job placement activities	20	4	11	35
Job recruitment and referrals	16	7	11	34
Job development	16	7	9	32
Assistive technology and workplace accommodations	8	9	15	32
Job retention training	9	10	10	29
On-the-job training	8	10	11	29
Support and services to employers of people with disabilities	6	11	11	28
Occupational or vocational training	12	9	6	27
Work experience	11	6	9	26
Vocational rehabilitation	11	7	6	24
Supported employment	3	9	12	24
Entrepreneurship training and support	3	6	13	22
Assistance in earning a high school diploma or its equivalent	3	5	12	20
Remedial academic, english language skills, or basic adult literacy	4	4	9	17
Tax expenditures	1	1		2

Number of programs

■ Service provided to more than 50 percent of program participants

▨ Service provided to less than 50 percent of program participants

☐ Service provided, but extent unknown

Source: GAO analysis of survey data.

Overlap was greatest in programs serving two distinct groups; specifically, we identified 19 programs that provided employment services to veterans and servicemembers (see fig. 3) and 5 programs that provided employment services to students and young adults (see fig. 4). In addition, 7 programs did not limit eligibility to any particular group and therefore potentially overlapped with these and other programs in our scope (see fig. 5). For example, 17 of the 19 programs that limit eligibility to veterans and servicemembers reported providing job-readiness skills. At the same time, any veteran or servicemember could receive these services from 5 of the 7 programs that did not limit eligibility to any particular population. The remaining 14 programs limited eligibility to other specific groups or types of disabilities, such as SSA disability beneficiaries, or people who are blind or visually impaired. For a complete list of programs, their objectives, and eligibility requirements, see appendix IV. For a list of programs, populations they serve, and the services they reported providing, see appendix V.

Figure 3: Selected Employment Services Reported to Be Provided by 19 Programs Limiting Eligibility to Veterans, Servicemembers, and/or Their Families, Fiscal Year 2010

Service	More than 50%	Less than 50%	Extent unknown	Total
Assistance earning a high school diploma or its equivalent	1	1	5	7
Assistive technology and workplace accommodations	6	3	3	12
Employment counseling, assessment, and case management	11	4	1	16
Employment-related information dissemination	9	7	2	18
Entrepreneurship training and support	2	1	6	9
Job development	11	3	1	15
Job readiness skills	12	2	3	17
Job recruitment and referrals	11	2	3	16
Job retention training	5	5	2	12
Job search/job placement activities	11	1	4	16
Occupational/vocational training	6	5	1	12
On-the-job training	5	5	2	12
Remedial academic, English language skills, or basic adult literacy	2	1	3	6
Support/services to employers of people with disabilities	5	5	3	13
Supported employment	2	5	3	10
Tax expenditures	1	1		2
Vocational rehabilitation	4	6	1	11
Work experience	5	3	4	12

Number of programs

■ Service provided to more than 50 percent of program participants

▨ Service provided to less than 50 percent of program participants

□ Service provided, but extent unknown

Source: GAO analysis of survey data

GAO-12-677 Employment for People with Disabilities

Figure 4: Selected Employment Services Reported to Be Provided by Five Programs Limiting Eligibility to Students, Transition-aged Youth, and/or Young Adults, Fiscal Year 2010

Service	Values
Assistance earning a high school diploma or its equivalent	1 / 3 / 4
Assistive technology and workplace accommodations	3
Employment counseling, assessment, and case management	2 / 1 / 1 / 4
Employment-related information dissemination	2 / 2 / 4
Entrepreneurship training and support	2
Job development	1 / 2 / 3
Job readiness skills	1 / 3 / 4
Job recruitment and referrals	1 / 3 / 4
Job retention training	3
Job search/job placement activities	1 / 3 / 4
Occupational/vocational training	1 / 2 / 3
On-the-job training	3
Remedial academic, English language skills, or basic adult literacy	1 / 2 / 3
Support/services to employers of people with disabilities	1 / 1 / 2
Supported employment	1
Tax expenditures	0
Vocational rehabilitation	1
Work experience	2 / 2 / 4

Number of programs (axis: 0, 3, 6, 9, 12, 15, 18)

Legend:
- Service provided to more than 50 percent of program participants
- Service provided to less than 50 percent of program participants
- Service provided, but extent unknown

Source: GAO analysis of survey data.

Figure 5: Selected Employment Services Reported to Be Provided by Seven Programs That Serve All People with Disabilities, Fiscal Year 2010

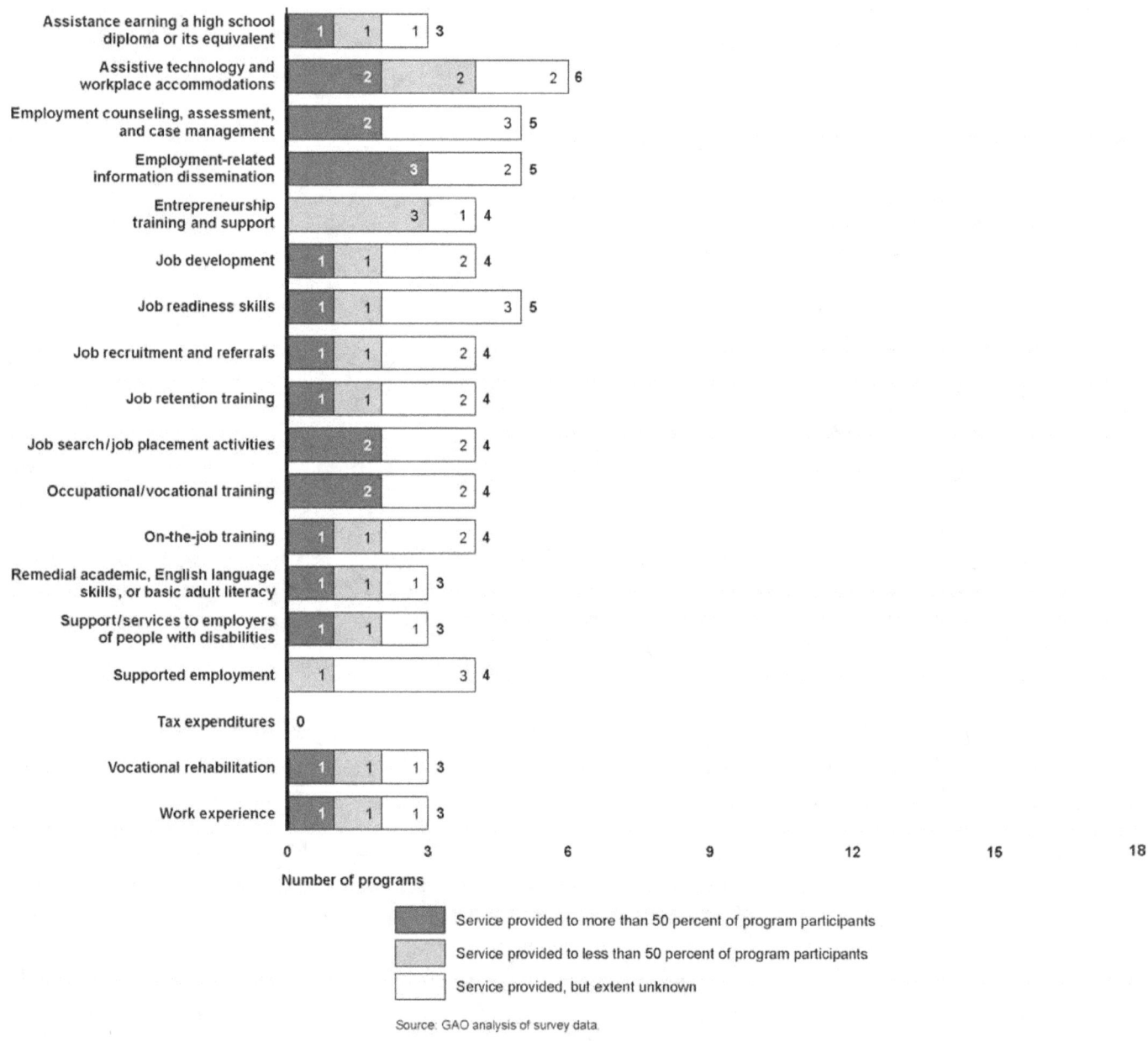

Source: GAO analysis of survey data.

The Potential for Duplication in Services May Be Low, but Administrative Inefficiencies Are Likely With Multiple Programs

While many programs reported providing similar services to similar populations, some programs have less potential for duplication—providing the same services to the same beneficiaries—than others. Some overlapping programs have specific eligibility requirements that make duplication less likely. For example, the Department of Veterans Affairs' (VA) Compensated Work Therapy and Vocational Rehabilitation and Employment (VR&E) programs both reported providing vocational rehabilitation and a number of other similar employment services to veterans with disabilities. However, the work therapy program targets veterans with mental illness or other severe disabilities who are patients in VA medical centers, whereas the VR&E program serves veterans with all types of disabilities. In addition, unlike the work therapy program, the VR&E program requires that a veteran's disability be connected to his or her military service.[15] In another example, the Workforce Recruitment Program, jointly administered by Labor and the Department of Defense, is the only one of the five youth programs that reported limiting eligibility to college students or recent graduates with disabilities.

On the other hand, we identified three programs—Labor's Workforce Investment Act (WIA) Youth, YouthBuild, and Registered Apprenticeship for Youth and Young Adults with Disabilities programs—that are potentially available to any youth with disabilities between the ages of 16 and 21 (see table 2) and reported offering many similar services, such as job readiness skills, on-the-job training, and assistance in obtaining a high school diploma.[16] Despite their similarities, Labor officials told us these programs employ different strategies for providing services. For example, the YouthBuild program focuses on helping youth earn their high-school equivalency degree while learning job skills by building affordable housing for homeless and low-income people, whereas the WIA Youth program is broader in that it focuses on more than construction skills and serves a larger population. The apprenticeship program is a small, 3-year pilot

---

[15]In addition to differences in eligibility requirements, VA officials reported that the types of services differ between the two programs. Compensated Work Therapy provides support with entry into employment at the veteran's current level of functioning, whereas VR&E provides career-level services, including training at a college, vocational, technical, or business school; on-the-job training; and nonpaid work experience to prepare veterans for entry into careers. VR&E also provides an independent living program, which is not available through the Compensated Work Therapy program.

[16]As shown in table 2, the programs have different age ranges for eligibility, but all allow eligible youth between the ages of 16 and 21 to participate.

program in two states administered in partnership with state-organized apprenticeship agencies to place young adults with disabilities in registered apprenticeships in the construction and health care fields. Labor officials said that case managers may refer a participant from the WIA Youth program to the YouthBuild program, for example, if they are interested in learning construction skills. However, it is difficult to determine the extent to which these different strategies reduce or prevent potential duplication in services among these programs.

Table 2: Reported Eligibility Requirements for Labor's Three Programs Limiting Eligibility to Students, Transition-age Youth, and/or Young Adults

Program name	Reported eligibility requirements
WIA Youth	Youth, ages 14 to 21, with a low personal or family income who also meet one or more of the following criteria: • deficient in basic literacy skills, • school dropout, • homeless, • runaway, • foster child, • pregnant or a parent, • an offender, or • requires additional assistance to complete their education or secure and hold employment. Up to 5 percent of youth participants in a local area do not have to meet the income criterion if they meet one of the following criteria: • school dropout; • basic skills deficient; • are one or more grade levels below the grade level appropriate to the individual's age; • pregnant or parenting; • possess one or more disabilities, including learning disabilities; • homeless or runaway; • offender; or • face serious barriers to employment as identified by the local board.
YouthBuild	Youth ages 16 through 24 and a member of a disadvantaged population, such as: • low-income, • foster care (including youth aging out of foster care), • youth offender, • youth with a disability, • child of an incarcerated parent, • high school dropout, or • migrant youth.

Program name	Reported eligibility requirements
Registered Apprenticeship for Youth and Young Adults with Disabilities	Youth and young adults with disabilities ages 16 through 27

Source: GAO analysis of survey data.

Note: Another Labor program, Job Corps, also generally serves youth and has similar eligibility requirements to WIA Youth and YouthBuild programs. However, eligible people with disabilities can apply to participate in the program at any age. Therefore, we did not include Job Corps as a program that limits eligibility to students, youth, and young adults.

Another factor affecting the potential for duplication is resource levels, in that some overlapping programs lack the capacity to serve all who apply, thereby reducing the potential for duplication in services. Six of the 45 programs reported having a waiting list for services (see table 3). Three of these programs reported serving only people with disabilities. Individuals who are on a waiting list for one program may be eligible to receive services from another program. For example, Labor officials told us that individuals waiting for VR services could be referred to one-stop career centers for services.[17]

Table 3: Programs Reporting Waiting Lists

Waiting list	Number of programs
Yes	6 programs • Computer/Electronic Accommodations Program (Department of Defense)[a] • VR program[a,b] (Education) • Job Corps (Labor) • Work Opportunity Tax Credit[c] (Labor/Internal Revenue Service) • Community Service Employment for Older Americans (Labor) • Compensated Work Therapy program (VA)[a]
No	26 programs
Don't know	6 programs
Not applicable	7 programs

Source: GAO analysis of survey data.

[17] In commenting on our report, Education noted that state VR agencies that are unable to serve all eligible individuals must give priority to those with the most significant disabilities. Individuals with less significant disabilities may be referred to other WIA partner programs. Likewise, other WIA programs may refer individuals with disabilities or suspected disabilities to VR agencies because of their capacity to provide specialized services.

Even when the potential for duplication of services is low, there may be inefficiencies associated with operating two or more separate programs that provide similar services to similar populations. For example, in its budget requests for fiscal years 2012 and 2013, Education proposed consolidating two smaller programs in our scope—the Migrant and Seasonal Farmworker and Supported Employment State Grants programs—into its larger VR program. Education proposed this consolidation in order to reduce duplication of effort and administrative costs, streamline program administration at the federal and local levels, and improve accountability.

Among the 19 programs that serve servicemembers and veterans, we identified two programs—Labor's Disabled Veterans' Outreach and Local Veterans' Employment Representatives programs—that provide similar services at similar locations, potentially by the same staff members. Both programs reported that they provided job search and placement services to veterans with disabilities, among other similar services. Labor officials said that the veterans' employment representatives were intended to reach out to employers and the disabled veterans' outreach specialists were intended to work with job seekers. However, as we reported in May 2007, staff often performed the same roles in one-stop career centers and, in some cases, the roles were carried out by the same staff member.[18] A recent law gave states the flexibility—subject to the approval of the Secretary of Labor—to consolidate these two programs in order to promote more efficient provision of services. Labor officials noted that the agency is in the process of developing criteria and procedures for making determinations on consolidations. The law also requires the Secretary of Labor to conduct audits to ensure that the veterans' employment representatives and the outreach specialists are performing their required

---

[18]GAO, *Veterans' Employment and Training Service: Labor Could Improve Information on Reemployment Services, Outcomes, and Program Impact*, GAO-07-594 (Washington, D.C.: May 24, 2007).

duties, and officials told us that they are in the process of defining the requirements and protocols for these audits.[19]

In another example, SSA administers two separate statutorily mandated programs—the State Vocational Rehabilitation Cost Reimbursement and the Ticket to Work programs—that perform similar functions in that they provide funding for employment supports to serve SSA disability beneficiaries. The Cost Reimbursement program reimburses state VR agencies when they help disability beneficiaries find jobs and earn above a certain threshold (known as substantial gainful activity) for 9 months.[20] The Ticket to Work program, established more than a decade after the Cost Reimbursement program, also provides funding to service providers (including, in some instances, VR agencies), when they help SSA disability beneficiaries achieve employment outcomes; retain employment; and whenever possible, support long-term financial independence.[21] State VR agencies can decide, on a case-by-case basis, whether to accept payments under the Ticket to Work or the Cost Reimbursement programs, but they may not receive payment under both programs at the same time for the same beneficiary. A senior SSA official noted that the Ticket to Work and Cost Reimbursement programs were both created to address a concern that VR and other workforce programs were not adequately serving SSA disability beneficiaries, given the severity of their disabilities. In addition, the official noted that both programs were intended, in part, to achieve cost savings by helping SSA disability beneficiaries achieve self-sufficiency and reduce or eliminate their reliance on disability benefits or payments. However, SSA officials also pointed out that the Ticket to Work program was intended, in part, to provide beneficiaries more choices in receiving employment services beyond those provided by VR agencies. In addition, officials noted that

[19]VOW to Hire Heroes Act of 2011, Pub. L. No. 112-56, § 241, 125 Stat. 712, 728.

[20]42 U.S.C. §§ 422(d) and 1382d(d); 20 C.F.R. §§ 404.2101 and 416.2201. Under thresholds set annually by SSA, individuals are considered engaged in substantial gainful activity if they had earnings in 2012 above $1,010 per month for nonblind beneficiaries and $1,690 per month for blind beneficiaries.

[21]42 U.S.C. § 1320b-19; 20 C.F.R. §§ 411.100 – 411.730. Specifically, the Ticket to Work program provides funding for SSA disability beneficiaries to receive employment services, vocational rehabilitation services, or other services to help them obtain and retain employment and reduce their dependency on benefits or payments. Individuals may receive services from SSA-approved public or private providers, known as employment networks, or traditional state VR agencies.

the two programs provide a continuum of services—VR agencies provide more intensive, up-front services to help beneficiaries enter or return to work, while employment networks under the Ticket to Work program can provide longer-term supports to help beneficiaries stay at work.

Officials Surveyed Reported Limited Coordination across All Programs

Coordination could help mitigate the potential for duplication among fragmented programs, but officials we surveyed reported limited coordination among the 45 programs in our scope. In our survey, we asked respondents to indicate whether their program coordinated with any of the other programs receiving our survey. In 13 percent of cases, two programs mutually reported coordinating with each other. However, in most cases, respondents either reported not coordinating or inconsistently reported coordinating with other programs (see table 4). For example, although VA's VR&E program reported coordinating with Labor's Veterans Workforce Investment Program and Disabled Veterans Outreach Program, only one of the two Labor programs—the Disabled Veterans Outreach Program—reported coordinating with the VA program. Officials explained that, in some cases, federal-level program staff responding to our survey may not be aware of coordination taking place at the state and local levels. Further, although the rate of mutual coordination reported is low among all the programs in our scope, programs that have different missions or serve different populations may not be expected to coordinate with one another. For instance, Labor's Senior Community Service Employment Program supports part-time work opportunities for low-income senior citizens, and therefore may not need to coordinate with Department of Defense transition programs—such as Operation Warfighter—that help servicemembers returning to civilian life gain employment experience.

Table 4: Coordination Reported by All Programs in Our Scope

Both programs reported coordinating	Both programs reported that they did not coordinate	Programs disagreed or did not know whether they coordinate
13%	44%	43%

Source: GAO analysis of survey data.

In order to better understand our survey results, we held more detailed discussions about coordination efforts with six selected programs that serve only people with disabilities:

- Assistive Technology State Grant program (Education)[22]

- Disability Employment Initiative (Labor)

- State Vocational Rehabilitation Cost Reimbursement Program (SSA)[23]

- Ticket to Work program (SSA)

- VR program (Education)

- Work Incentives Planning and Assistance program (SSA)

Officials cited more consistent coordination among these programs. In response to our survey, all six programs had mutually reported coordinating with the Ticket to Work and the VR programs. This is perhaps not surprising, given that the VR program reported serving the largest number of people with disabilities and the Ticket to Work program is closely related to the VR program.

Although not all of the six programs mutually reported coordination, federal program officials noted that a significant amount of coordination occurs at the state and local levels where services are delivered. Labor officials reported that its Disability Employment Initiative grantees at the state and local level have established Integrated Resource Teams, which include representatives from a number of programs—including the VR program, the Assistive Technology State Grant program, and other state and local programs—to leverage all available resources for individual clients. To further encourage local coordination, Labor recently issued guidance to state and local workforce agencies outlining ways in which programs housed in one-stop career centers can coordinate with providers under SSA's Ticket to Work program.[24] Labor issued similar

---

[22]In commenting on a draft of this report, Education noted that the services provided by the Assistive Technology State Grant program may facilitate employment or contribute to obtaining employment, but it is not exclusively an employment program.

[23]As noted previously, SSA's State Vocational Cost Reimbursement Program does not directly serve individuals with disabilities. Rather, it reimburses state VR agencies when they help disability beneficiaries find jobs and earn above a certain threshold for 9 months.

[24]Department of Labor, *Training and Employment Notice No. 6-11: Increasing the Public Workforce Development System's Participation in the Ticket to Work (TTW) Program for Disability Beneficiaries* (Aug. 24, 2011).

guidance listing available resources to help beneficiaries obtain assistive technology, including Education's Assistive Technology State Grant program and SSA's Ticket to Work program.[25]

Agency officials also described efforts to increase coordination more broadly among programs that support employment for people with disabilities. For example, in 2008, Education and SSA established the Partnership Plus initiative, which is intended to provide a seamless approach to vocational services for people with disabilities. Individuals who need intensive employment services, such as education or training, can receive them first through the VR program, and then transition to an employment network under Ticket to Work for job retention services, or other ongoing services and supports to maintain employment and increase earnings. In addition, officials described a new initiative that coordinates programs and leverages resources from Education, the Department of Health and Human Services, Labor, and SSA, and aims to help youth receiving Supplemental Security Income to transition successfully to higher education or employment by working with the entire family to provide supports necessary to reduce barriers and improve outcomes.[26]

Officials from selected programs reported facing a number of challenges in coordinating with each other. First, officials noted that coordination can be challenging because programs are governed by separate statutes and regulations containing different definitions and program requirements. One official noted that aligning definitions of disability in statute would be helpful to ensure programs established by WIA and the Rehabilitation Act are complementary. In interviews with our six selected programs, officials from each reported that individual programs lack the resources, both in terms of funding and staff time, to pursue coordination with one another. Finally, one official indicated that interagency working groups may have limited effectiveness. He said that, in general, coordination could be more effective if programs had a set of outcomes they were expected to collectively achieve and were given the authority to work together to do

---

[25]Department of Labor, *Training and Employment Notice No.16-11: Availability of Assistive Technology (AT) Resources for Persons with Disabilities* (Nov. 15, 2011).

[26]The Promoting Readiness of Minors in Supplemental Security Income (PROMISE) initiative was first proposed in the President's 2012 budget and therefore not within the scope of this engagement, but demonstrates ongoing efforts for greater coordination among federal agencies.

GAO-12-677 Employment for People with Disabilities

so—including the authority to waive requirements that present barriers— and given funding to support such collaboration. This is consistent with concerns raised in our 2010 forum on employment for people with disabilities, where participants noted that past interagency coordination efforts have not been very successful at achieving significant change because they have lacked sufficient authority, accountability, or resources.[27]

Programs Tracked Varying Outcome Measures, and Little Is Known About Program Effectiveness

Programs Reported Tracking Varying Employment Outcomes for People with Disabilities

Coordination efforts can be enhanced when agencies work toward a common goal, yet outcome measures varied across programs and not all programs reported outcomes specifically for people with disabilities. Given a list of typical employment measures, 32 of the 45 programs reported tracking at least one employment measure specifically for people with disabilities.[28] The measures varied across programs, but the measures most commonly tracked were "participants who enter employment" (28 programs) and "participants' employment retention" (18 programs). Some programs reported tracking other indicators, such as quality of life. For instance, both VA's VR&E program and Education's Helen Keller National Center track the number of participants who are able to live independently or in less-restrictive residential programs. The remaining 13 programs did not report tracking any employment-related outcomes for people with disabilities, in part because they have a broader mission. For instance, Department of Health and Human Services officials reported that states are required to identify various performance measures in their applications for the Medicaid 1915(c) Home and Community-Based Services Waivers and the 1915(i) State Plan Home

---

[27]GAO, *Highlights of a Forum: Actions that Could Increase Work Participation for Adults with Disabilities*, GAO-10-812SP (Washington, D.C.: July 2010).

[28]Nineteen of these programs reported limiting eligibility to people with disabilities.

and Community-Based Services related to participants' health and welfare overall, but are not required to measure employment-related outcome measures because both programs provide a broad range of health care and other services beyond employment-related services.[29] See Figure 6 for the number of programs tracking specific outcome measures.

Figure 6: Measures Reported by Programs to Track Employment Outcomes for People with Disabilities

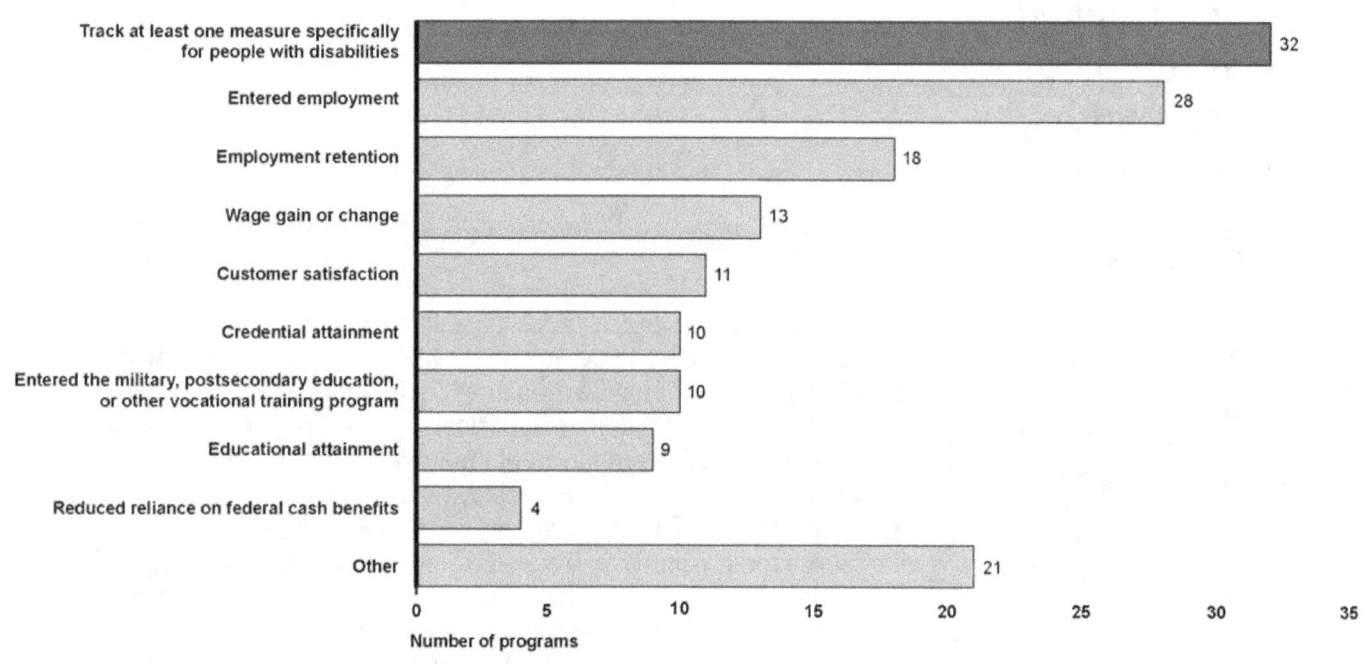

Number of programs

Source: GAO analysis of survey data.

Despite some similarities in programs' outcome measures, it can be difficult to compare relative performance due to variation across programs in the type and severity of participants' disabilities. Just over half (24) of the 45 programs reported targeting or giving priority to people with significant or severe disabilities for whom it may be challenging to achieve

[29]Both may be used to permit states to provide long-term care services, including employment-related services like supported employment, in home and community based settings as an alternative to institutional care under the Medicaid program. 42 U.S.C. § 1396n(c) and (i).

GAO-12-677 Employment for People with Disabilities

positive employment outcomes.[30] Further, some programs may use different thresholds for their employment outcome measures. For example, although 28 programs reported tracking "participants who enter employment," officials told us that some programs may consider just a few hours of paid work per week as an employment outcome, while others set a higher bar and require a participant to be working at a level that would allow them to become self-sufficient and eliminate their dependence on federal disability benefits.

Some Programs Have Conducted Evaluations, but Few Have Measured Their Impact

Little is known about the effectiveness of the programs we identified as supporting employment for people with disabilities because only about one-quarter reported having a performance review. Ten of the 45 programs in our scope reported that a review or study had been conducted to evaluate their program's performance.[31] The studies varied in methodology, and many examined program outcomes and proposed ways to improve services, but fell short of determining whether outcomes were a direct result of program activities. (See app. VII for programs that reported performance reviews.) For example, the Department of Agriculture's AgrAbility program conducted a review of its activities between 1991 and 2011 that found that 11,000 clients had been served, and that 88 percent of those clients continued to be engaged in farm or ranch activities. However, this study did not determine whether other factors may have contributed to participants' positive outcomes. Likewise, a 2009 study evaluated aspects of Labor's YouthBuild program—such as recruitment and enrollment procedures, educational and vocational services, and case management—to understand similarities and

[30]Programs may have a variety of definitions for "severe" or "significant" disability. Our survey instrument did not specify a definition, but we offered an example of one agency's definition of an individual with a "significant disability": "an individual who has a severe physical or mental impairment that seriously limits functional capabilities, such as mobility, communication, or self-care."

[31]Officials from two additional programs reported conducting evaluation studies, but one had not been completed at the time of our survey and the other was a GAO report that was not an evaluation of program performance. In commenting on our draft report, Labor noted that most of its programs have been or are being evaluated. Starting in fiscal year 2010, the agency stated that it expanded its evaluation activities with the creation of a Chief Evaluation Office. Of the 10 programs in our scope that reported having an impact evaluation or another review or study to evaluate program performance, three were Labor programs.

differences across grantees, but the study did not attempt to discern the effect of the program on participants' employment.[32]

Only one program in our scope—Labor's Job Corps program—reported having a study that meets the criteria of an impact study. Impact studies examine what would have happened in the absence of a program to isolate its impact from other factors. Many researchers consider impact studies to be the best method for determining the extent to which a program is responsible for participant outcomes, but these studies can be challenging to conduct. However, there are sometimes opportunities for agencies to assess impacts without conducting full-scale impact studies. As an example, Education officials noted that it may be more feasible to conduct a rigorous study to evaluate the impact of providing enhanced services over regular services, rather than the impact of providing services over providing no services at all. The Job Corps impact study compared the outcomes of participants in the program to outcomes of a comparable group of individuals who did not participate in the program. The study concluded that, although there were no long-term program impacts on earnings for many Job Corps participants, the program generated earnings gains for participants between the ages of 20 and 24, who may be more highly motivated and disciplined.

Reports for two additional programs that were excluded from our scope—SSA's Youth Transition Demonstration and the Mental Health Treatment Study programs[33]—met the criteria for impact studies. Each of the programs was a demonstration project that included an impact study to determine whether the program produced positive outcomes. The Youth Transition Demonstration Project had interim impact studies for three project sites.[34] The studies concluded that, while the program did result in greater use of services to promote employment, it did not impact the employment of participants from two out of three project sites during the

---

[32]Social Policy Research Associates, *Evaluation of the YouthBuild Youth Offender Grants Final Report* (May 2009). YouthBuild does not limit eligibility to people with disabilities. This report did not focus specifically on youth with disabilities, but on outcomes for all youth offenders participating in the program.

[33]Although we surveyed both programs, we excluded them from our data analysis for this report because they were demonstration studies that had ended by December 2011. See appendix II for more information.

[34]Youth Transition Demonstration–Interim Reports, http://www.ssa.gov/disabilityresearch/interimreports.html, accessed June 13, 2012.

GAO-12-677 Employment for People with Disabilities

1-year follow-up period.[35] The program also did not impact the education or income of participants from the three project sites during the 1-year follow-up period. The Mental Health Treatment Study program also published an impact study, which concluded that there was significant improvement in the 24-month employment rate for the group receiving services (61 percent versus 40 percent employment for the control group).[36]

Finally, agencies may have published or initiated impact studies after responding to our survey. For instance, officials at Labor notified us of two impact studies currently being planned or underway, for the YouthBuild program and for the Disability Employment Initiative.

Concluding Observations

The number of programs providing similar employment services to people with disabilities—and the range of requirements and approaches they entail—raises questions about the current structure of federal disability programs. In fact, several of the programs we identified were created in order to help people with disabilities navigate this fragmented system. Efforts such as Education's proposed consolidation of several smaller programs into its VR program also indicate an awareness of the need to simplify the system and increase effectiveness and ease of use. In our February 2012 report on duplication and overlap in government programs, we suggested that OMB continue to work with executive agencies that administer overlapping programs to identify any opportunities for cost savings or streamlining, such as program consolidation. We continue to believe that such a review could result in more effective and efficient delivery of services to help people with disabilities obtain and retain employment.

---

[35]One study estimated that the City University of New York's project increased participation in paid employment during the 1-year follow-up period. However, the study explains that this may be because site participants took part in summer employment through the project. Mathematica Policy Research, The Social Security Administration's Youth Transition Demonstration Projects: Interim Report on the City University of New York's Project, (April 2011). Available at http://www.mathematica-mpr.com/publications/pdfs/disability/SSA_YTD_CUNY.pdf, accessed June 15, 2012.

[36] Westat, Mental Health Treatment Study Final Report, (July 2011), available at http://www.ssa.gov/disabilityresearch/documents/MHTS_Final_Report_508.pdf, accessed June 15, 2012.

We identified limited coordination among programs that provide employment support for people with disabilities, which may exacerbate the potential for duplication among fragmented programs. In addition, many programs have not evaluated their programs for effectiveness, and little is known about effectiveness overall, such that policymakers have limited information to help them make informed decisions on allocating scarce resources. In our February 2012 report, we noted that OMB should consider establishing governmentwide goals related to employment of people with disabilities, with agencies establishing related outcome measures. We continue to believe that setting common goals across programs that support employment for people with disabilities could help spur greater coordination and more efficient and economical service delivery in overlapping program areas, and plan to follow up with OMB on its progress with respect to both of the actions we suggested in our February 2012 report.

Agency Comments and Our Evaluation

We provided copies of our draft report to the nine federal agencies that administer programs within the scope of this report for comment. The AbilityOne Commission; the Departments of Defense and Health and Human Services; and the Internal Revenue Service had no comments. The Departments of Education, Labor, and Veterans Affairs, and SSA provided technical comments, which we incorporated into the report, as appropriate. The Departments of Agriculture, Education, and Labor also provided written comments, which are reproduced in appendixes VIII, IX, and X, respectively.

In its comments, the Department of Agriculture noted that it generally concurred with our findings. Education provided additional information and examples of how its VR program coordinates services at the state and local level that were not fully described in our report. For example, Education noted that the program coordinates at the state level with each state's workforce investment system, and state VR agencies have staff who provide a variety of education, training, and rehabilitation services to one-stop career center customers with disabilities. Education also stated that the capacity of the VR program to provide and coordinate a wide range of individualized services to achieve employment outcomes for individuals with disabilities—particularly individuals with significant disabilities—is not duplicated by any other program.

Labor generally expressed concern that we found fragmentation among the programs we examined, noting that our definition of fragmentation is broad. We continue to believe that fragmentation—defined as more than one federal agency (or organization within an agency) being involved in the same broad area of national need—exists among the 45 programs we identified across nine federal agencies. As we have noted, unless programs coordinate effectively, fragmentation could lead to inefficient use of scarce resources, confuse program beneficiaries, and ultimately, limit the overall effectiveness of the federal effort. Labor also expressed concern about our statement that certain youth programs with similar eligibility requirements present a greater risk of potential duplication than other programs, noting that we did not consider the unique characteristics of the programs, such as the individual services provided, the program design used, or the populations served. We did consider such factors and provided some information in our report about the different ways these programs serve the youth population. However, we were unable to determine the extent to which these factors reduce the potential for duplication.

Further, while Labor acknowledged that it is important to minimize duplication and maximize efficiency, it noted that some overlap is necessary and appropriate to ensure that all participants receive comprehensive employment and training services. We agree that, in some instances, overlap among programs involved in providing services to similar populations may be appropriate. However, we continue to believe there is value in examining overlapping programs to identify opportunities for streamlining and coordination to more efficiently provide services.

Labor also pointed out that several of its programs included in the scope of our study were created to serve all job-seekers rather than specifically to provide employment support for people with disabilities. Labor also noted that, rather than being seen as duplicative or undesirable, service integration and diversity of design are important for achieving inclusion of people with disabilities consistent with what Congress envisioned. We included such programs to provide a more comprehensive picture of the services and supports available to help people with disabilities stay at work or return to work. We did not label any given program as duplicative or undesirable, but noted that, in some cases, having many programs serving similar populations may result in administrative inefficiencies.

We are sending copies of this report to the AbilityOne Commission; the Departments of Agriculture, Defense, Education, Health and Human Services, Labor, and Veterans Affairs; the Internal Revenue Service; and SSA. In addition, the report is available at no charge on the GAO website at http://www.gao.gov.

If you or your staff have any questions about this report, please contact me at (202) 512-7215 or bertonid@gao.gov. Contact points for our Offices of Congressional Relations and Public Affairs may be found on the last page of this report. GAO staff who made key contributions to this report are listed in appendix XI.

Daniel Bertoni, Director
Education, Workforce, and Income Security

List of Committees

The Honorable Debbie Stabenow
Chairwoman
The Honorable Pat Roberts
Ranking Member
Committee on Agriculture, Nutrition and Forestry
United States Senate

The Honorable Carl Levin
Chairman
The Honorable John McCain
Ranking Member
Committee on Armed Services
United States Senate

The Honorable Max Baucus
Chairman
The Honorable Orrin G. Hatch
Ranking Member
Committee on Finance
United States Senate

The Honorable Tom Harkin
Chairman
The Honorable Michael B. Enzi
Ranking Member
Committee on Health, Education, Labor, and Pensions
United States Senate

The Honorable Joseph I. Lieberman
Chairman
The Honorable Susan M. Collins
Ranking Member
Committee on Homeland Security and Governmental Affairs
United States Senate

The Honorable Patty Murray
Chairman
The Honorable Richard Burr
Ranking Member
Committee on Veterans' Affairs
United States Senate

The Honorable Tom Harkin
Chairman
The Honorable Richard Shelby
Ranking Member
Subcommittee on Labor, Health and Human Services,
    Education, and Related Agencies
Committee on Appropriations
United States Senate

The Honorable Frank D. Lucas
Chairman
The Honorable Collin Peterson
Ranking Member
Committee on Agriculture
House of Representatives

The Honorable Howard P. McKeon
Chairman
The Honorable Adam Smith
Ranking Member
Committee on Armed Services
House of Representatives

The Honorable John Kline
Chairman
The Honorable George Miller
Ranking Member
Committee on Education and the Workforce
House of Representatives

The Honorable Fred Upton
Chairman
The Honorable Henry A. Waxman
Ranking Member
Committee on Energy and Commerce
House of Representatives

The Honorable Darrell E. Issa
Chairman
The Honorable Elijah Cummings
Ranking Member
Committee on Oversight and Government Reform
House of Representatives

The Honorable Jeff Miller
Chairman
The Honorable Bob Filner
Ranking Member
Committee on Veterans' Affairs
House of Representatives

The Honorable Dave Camp
Chairman
The Honorable Sander Levin
Ranking Member
Committee on Ways and Means
House of Representatives

The Honorable Denny Rehberg
Chairman
The Honorable Rosa DeLauro
Ranking Member
Subcommittee on Labor, Health and Human Services,
Education, and Related Agencies
Committee on Appropriations
House of Representatives

Appendix I: Objectives, Scope, and Methodology

Our objectives were to examine: (1) to what extent do federal programs that support employment for people with disabilities provide similar services to similar populations and (2) to what extent has the effectiveness of programs that support employment for people with disabilities been measured? The interim results for this report were included in our February 2012 report on duplication and overlap in government programs.[1]

Identifying Programs that Provide Employment-Related Services to People with Disabilities

We determined that programs included in the scope of our work should meet two sets of criteria. Specifically, they should: (1) be targeted to people with disabilities or their employers and (2) have provided specific employment and training services in fiscal year 2010.[2] See figure 7 for a detailed description of both sets of criteria.

---

[1]GAO-12-342SP.

[2]We excluded Recovery Act programs; loans (such as Pell Grants and federal student loans); civil protection and legal services (such as nondiscrimination requirements and protection and advocacy programs); research; personal assistant services (such as independent living); training for professionals who work with people with disabilities; federal employment and contracting preferences; and programs whose objectives do not explicitly include helping job seekers enhance their job skills, find job opportunities, obtain, or retain employment, including general education programs.

Figure 7: Criteria for Including Programs within Our Scope

Programs must meet one or more of the following criteria:

1. people with disabilities are **specifically mentioned** in a program's authorizing legislation as a targeted group,

2. people are **eligible for the program wholly because of a disability,**

3. people are **eligible for the program partially because of a disability,**

4. people with disabilities are given **special consideration** in eligibility determinations,

5. people with disabilities are given **priority in service,** or

6. **employers** of people with disabilities are a target population

+

Programs must provide one or more of the following primary types of assistance:

1. **Direct employment services** to individuals (including vocational rehabilitation, job training, job placement, job acquisition and retention)

2. **Infrastructure** support

3. **Recruitment** and referral services

4. **Information dissemination**

5. **Case management**

6. **Tax expenditures** related to workers with disabilities

7. **Entrepreneurship** training and support

8. **Assistive technology**

Source: GAO.

We identified and selected programs for inclusion in our review leveraging a variety of sources and a multi-step process. Specifically, we identified programs for potential inclusion using key terms to search the Catalog of Federal Domestic Assistance (CFDA), reviewing our previous work on related topics, and consulting with internal and external stakeholders. We then reviewed the programs' objectives and eligibility criteria from CFDA or program websites to determine if the program met our inclusion criteria. If key information, such as how a program focuses on people with disabilities or provides employment-related services, was incomplete or ambiguous, we kept the program in our preliminary list.

We sent our preliminary list of programs for validation to the 10 agencies that administer the programs. The agencies requested we add several programs to our list, and determined that others did not meet the criteria for inclusion. We held follow-up meetings with agency officials to clarify criteria, as appropriate. We determined that the two programs in our preliminary list administered by the Small Business Administration did not meet our criteria and thus we excluded the agency and the programs from our review.

Our validation process yielded a total of 56 programs administered by nine federal agencies. We surveyed these programs from August to October 2011. Based on agency responses and follow-up conversations, we omitted six surveyed programs because we found they did not meet the inclusion criteria.[3] We reported on 50 of those programs in our February 2012 report.[4]

For this final report, we have omitted an additional 7 programs and added 2 new programs, for a total of 45 programs. We omitted six programs that had ended as of April 2012, and one demonstration program—the Benefit Offset National Demonstration—that did not begin enrolling participants until January 2011. (See app. II for a list of programs we omitted.) In commenting on a draft of our February 2012 report and, later, in verifying data previously provided, Department of Defense officials requested that we add three programs that they believed to be within the scope of this review. After identifying the programs' employment services to people with disabilities, we determined that two—the Army Warrior Care and Transition and the Marines Wounded Warrior Regiment programs—met our criteria and thus were included in our analyses for this report.

We did not include or review programs that may have been created or revised to meet our inclusion criteria after fiscal year 2010.

Surveying Programs

We designed a web-based survey to collect information on program background, eligibility requirements and populations served, services,

---

[3]Specifically, we excluded: the Department of Health and Human Services' (HHS) Demonstration to Maintain Independence and Employment because program officials reported that the program was not funded in fiscal year 2010; the Department of Labor's (Labor) Homeless Veterans Reintegration Program and the Department of Veteran Affairs' Educational and Vocational Counseling program because program officials reported that the programs did not provide any special consideration to people with disabilities in eligibility determinations; the Section 1915(b) waivers program (HHS) and the Section 1115 Medicaid demonstration projects (HHS) because officials reported that the programs did not provide any of the employment-related services listed in the survey; and Disability Program Navigator (Labor) because officials reported that the program was a subprogram of another program included in our scope (Work Incentive Grants).

[4]GAO-12-342SP.

outcome measures, and budget information. In designing this survey, we reviewed our prior surveys used to collect similar information.[5] We pretested the survey with three programs to minimize errors that may arise from differences in how questions might be interpreted and ensure that response categories were appropriate.

From August through October 2011, we fielded the web-based survey of 56 federal programs that support employment for people with disabilities. Program representatives were identified by the agencies. Where programs were jointly administered by two or more federal agencies, we consulted with the agencies and asked them to designate one official to fill out the survey and respond to questions for that program. In March 2012, we fielded the web-based survey to two additional programs that were later determined to meet our inclusion criteria (Army Warrior Care and Transition Program and the Marine Corps Wounded Warrior Regiment, discussed earlier). We received completed questionnaires from 58 programs, for a 100 percent response rate.

Quality Assurance

We used standard descriptive statistics to analyze responses to the questionnaire. Because this was not a sample survey, there were no sampling errors. To minimize other types of errors, commonly referred to as nonsampling errors, and to enhance data quality, we employed recognized survey design practices in the development of the questionnaire and in the collection, processing, and analysis of the survey data. For instance, as previously mentioned, we pretested the questionnaire with program officials. We further reviewed the survey to ensure the ordering of survey sections was appropriate and that the questions within each section were clearly stated and easy to comprehend. To reduce nonresponse, another source of nonsampling error, we sent out e-mail reminder messages and made telephone calls to encourage officials to complete the survey.

---

[5]For example, we reviewed the survey used in the following GAO reports: *Multiple Employment and Training Programs: Providing Information on Colocating Services and Consolidating Administrative Structures Could Promote Efficiencies,* GAO-11-92 (Washington, D.C.: Jan. 13, 2011), and *Federal Disability Assistance: Wide Array of Programs Needs to Be Examined in Light of 21st Century Challenges,* GAO-05-626 (Washington, D.C.: June 2, 2005).

In reviewing the survey data, we performed automated checks to identify inconsistent answers. We further reviewed the data for missing, ambiguous, or illogical responses and followed up with agency officials when necessary to clarify their responses. In addition, we compared 2010 obligations data provided by survey respondents with data provided to us in a previous survey and with appropriations data from the Consolidated Federal Funds Report. Where obligations differed from the comparison sources by 10 percent or more, we contacted program officials to confirm reported data. Finally, in March and April 2012, we collected some additional data from agencies and verified select data collected during the initial survey. Because we updated selected data and the list of programs included in our analyses, some data in our analyses have changed since our February 2012 report. On the basis of our application of recognized survey design practices and follow-up procedures, we determined that the data were sufficiently reliable for our purposes. We did not conduct an independent legal analysis to verify the program information provided by survey respondents.

Survey Analysis

Fragmentation, Overlap, and Potential Duplication

We have defined fragmentation to be when more than one federal agency is involved in the same broad area of national need. To further expand on this definition, we used the survey responses to identify: the number of programs created in statute and variability in definitions of disability and the ways in which programs deliver supports (e.g., directly to individuals, or through federal, state, or local entities).

We have defined overlap to be instances where programs provide similar services to similar populations. To identify areas of potential overlap among programs that support employment for people with disabilities, we reviewed survey responses from agency officials. We analyzed responses to survey questions regarding any limitations in eligibility based on populations or disability.

We sorted the 45 programs into 4 groups:

1. Programs that limit eligibility to servicemembers and veterans (19 programs).[6]

2. Programs that limit eligibility to students, transition-age youth and/or young adults (5 programs).

3. Programs that limit eligibility to other populations or specific types of disabilities (14 programs).

4. Programs that serve all people with disabilities (7 programs).

We have defined duplication as when the same beneficiaries receive the same or similar services. Although fragmentation and overlap may indicate the potential for duplication, we did not identify actual duplication in programs that provide employment support to people with disabilities because (1) due to data limitations, we did not attempt an intensive data matching among our universe of programs to identify instances where programs were providing the same or similar services to the same beneficiaries, and (2) programs do not consistently collect information on beneficiaries.

Instead, we examined the potential for duplication by more closely examining the reported eligibility requirements among programs in our four groups.

Coordination

We asked survey respondents if their program coordinated with each of the other programs in our scope to reduce duplication and gaps and services. While we surveyed federal program officials, our survey question did not specify if we were requesting information on coordination at the federal level, or at the state and local level where services and supports may be delivered. We analyzed the data to identify mismatches in reported coordination. For example, we identified cases in which program A reported that they coordinated with program B, but program B did not report coordinating with program A.

To further understand the nature and challenges of coordination, we selected a subgroup of programs with which to hold further discussion on

---

[6]We combined programs serving servicemembers and those serving veterans because four programs reported serving both populations.

coordination. Specifically, we selected six programs—administered by three different agencies—that served only people with disabilities:

- Assistive Technology State Grant program [Department of Education (Education)]

- Disability Employment Initiative (a new program that replaced the Work Incentive Grants) [Department of Labor (Labor)]

- State Vocational Rehabilitation Cost Reimbursement Program [Social Security Administration (SSA)]

- Ticket to Work program (SSA)

- State Vocational Rehabilitation Services program (VR) (Education)

- Work Incentives Planning and Assistance program (SSA)

We interviewed agency representatives for each program regarding their coordination efforts, challenges to coordination, and factors that facilitate or create barriers to coordination.

Performance Evaluations: Impact Studies and Other Studies

We asked all survey respondents to provide information on any performance evaluations that have been completed since 2006 related to employment for people with disabilities for their program and to provide citations to those studies. We selected 2006 because studies conducted in the past 5 years were most likely to include services still offered by each program and be relevant to the employment market participants are currently facing. We reviewed the findings and conclusions of a total of 14 studies identified by programs in our scope to determine the elements of program performance that had been evaluated. Although programs identified a total of 18 program studies, 1 was not publicly available and 2 programs had identified a GAO report that had been published prior to 2006. In addition, we evaluated the methodology section of 11 of those studies, which were identified as impact studies by 7 programs, to determine if they met our criteria for an impact study—that is, the study provides an assessment of the net effect of a program by comparing program outcomes with an estimate of what would have happened in the absence of the program.

We conducted this performance audit from April 2011 through June 2012 in accordance with generally accepted government auditing standards.

Those standards require that we plan and perform the audit to obtain sufficient, appropriate evidence to provide a reasonable basis for our findings and conclusions based on our audit objectives. We believe that the evidence obtained provides a reasonable basis for our findings and conclusions based on our audit objectives.

Appendix II: Selected Survey Data from Programs That Have Ended Since Fiscal Year 2010

Program name (agency)	Number of people with disabilities receiving employment services (fiscal year 2010)	Services	Details on status
Medicaid Infrastructure Grant Program (Department of Health and Human Services)	Program did not provide data	• Employment-related information dissemination • Support services to employers of people with disabilities	The program, authorized for 11 years, expired at the close of fiscal year 2011.
Mental Health Treatment Study (SSA)	Program did not provide data[a]	• Employment counseling, assessment and case management • Assistance in earning a high school diploma or its equivalent • Job development • Job readiness skills • Job recruitment and referrals • Job retention training • Job search or placement activities • On-the-job training • Occupational or vocational training • Vocational rehabilitation • Supported employment • Remedial academic, English language skills, or adult literacy • Employment-related information dissemination • Entrepreneurship training and support • Assistive technology and workplace accommodation • Case management and nurse care coordinators	The study to test how better access to treatment and employment services would affect outcomes such as medical recovery, employment, and benefit receipt for Social Security Disability Insurance ended field operations on July 31, 2010. According to the agency's budget justification for fiscal year 2013, the project's funding continued and, going forward, the agency will focus on best practices in services to individuals with schizophrenia and affective disorder and track employment and benefit payments.

Program name (agency)	Number of people with disabilities receiving employment services (fiscal year 2010)	Services	Details on status
National Organization on Disability Wounded Warrior Career Demonstration Project (Department of Defense)	1,300	• Employment counseling, assessment and case management • Job development • Job readiness skills • Job recruitment and referrals • Job retention training • Job search or placement activities • Occupational or vocational training • Vocational rehabilitation • Supported employment • Remedial academic, English language skills, or adult literacy • Work experience • Employment-related information dissemination • Entrepreneurship training and support • Support services to employers of people with disabilities • Assistive technology and workplace accommodation • Funding may be provided to the veteran	This program, administered by the National Organization of Disability, provided services to wounded, ill, and injured U.S. Army personnel through a memorandum of agreement, which ended October, 2010.
Projects with Industry (Education)	5,454	• Employment counseling, assessment, and case management • Assistance in earning a high school diploma or its equivalent • Job development • Job readiness skills • Job recruitment and referrals • Job retention training • Job search or placement activities • Occupational or vocational training • Vocational rehabilitation • On-the-job training • Employment-related information dissemination • Support services to employers of people with disabilities • Assistive technology and workplace accommodation	The program was eliminated in the fiscal year 2011 appropriation.

GAO-12-677 Employment for People with Disabilities

Program name (agency)	Number of people with disabilities receiving employment services (fiscal year 2010)	Services	Details on status
Work Incentive Grant/ Disability Program Navigator (Labor)	Program did not provide data	Employment counseling, assessment and case management Employment-related information dissemination Entrepreneurship training and support Support services to employers of people with disabilities Assistive technology and workplace accommodation Medicaid services	The Work Incentives Grant funded the Disability Program Navigator Initiative. Both programs ended effective June 30, 2010. A new program, the Disability Employment Initiative, was informed by the best practices learned through the Work Incentive Grant/Disability Program Navigator initiative.
Youth Transition Demonstration Project (SSA)	1,290	Employment counseling, assessment and case management Assistance in earning a high school diploma or its equivalent Job development Job readiness skills Job recruitment and referrals Job retention training Job search or placement activities On-the-job training Remedial academic, English language skills, or adult literacy Work experience Employment-related information dissemination Entrepreneurship training and support Support services to employers of people with disabilities Assistive technology and workplace accommodation.	The program suspended services at the end of calendar year 2011. A 36-month evaluation of the impact of the program is scheduled to follow. Funding was approximately $1.35 million in fiscal years 2012 and 2013.

Sources: GAO survey and agency interviews.

[a]This program enrolled participants on a rolling basis between 2006 and 2009 and served 1,121 individuals over the course of the project.

GAO-12-677 Employment for People with Disabilities

Appendix III: Reported Program Obligations and Number of People with Disabilities Served

Program	Fiscal year 2010 obligation	Portion of fiscal year 2010 obligation for employment-related services and support for people with disabilities[a]	Number of people with disabilities provided employment services, fiscal year 2010
U.S. AbilityOne Commission			
AbilityOne Program	$5,380,775	$0	47,000
Department of Agriculture			
Assistive Technology Program for Farmers with Disabilities: AgrAbility Project	4,667,107	4,667,107	1,304
Department of Defense			
Air Force Warrior and Survivor Care	Data not available[b]	0	Data not available[b]
Army Warrior Care and Transition Program	1,374,360,000[c]	Data not available[b]	4,368[d]
Computer/Electronic Accommodations Program	8,847,404	8,847,404	11,775
Marine Corps Wounded Warrior Regiment	0	0	Data not available[b]
Marine Corps Wounded Warrior Intern Program	0	0	115[e]
Navy Safe Harbor Program	2,400,000	24,000	78[f]
Recovery Care Coordinator Program	3,825,960	0	Data not available[b]
Recovery Coordination Program – Operation Warfighter (Internships)	966,502	966,502	Data not available[b]
U.S. Special Operations Command Care Coalition	3,592,700	Data not available[b]	Data not available[b]
Department of Education			
American Indian Vocational Rehabilitation Services	42,822,202	42,822,202	8,395
Helen Keller National Center for Deaf-Blind Youths and Adults	9,181,000	9,181,000	1,576
Migrant and Seasonal Farmworkers[g]	2,197,283	2,197,283	137
Model Comprehensive Transition and Postsecondary Programs for Students with Intellectual Disabilities[g]	11,000,000	11,000,000	Data not available[b]
Randolph-Sheppard Vending Facility Program	0[h]	0	2,319
Rehabilitation Services Demonstration and Training Programs	11,601,000	5,800,000	Data not available[b]
Assistive Technology State Grant program	25,660,000	Data not available[b]	5,882
Supported Employment State Grants[g]	28,889,190	28,889,190	35,668
State Vocational Rehabilitation Services	3,041,746,049	3,041,746,049	1,011,395
Department of Health and Human Services			
1915(c) Home and Community Based Services Waiver	Data not available[b]	Data not available[b]	Data not available[b]

Program	Fiscal year 2010 obligation	Portion of fiscal year 2010 obligation for employment-related services and support for people with disabilities[a]	Number of people with disabilities provided employment services, fiscal year 2010
1915(i) State Plan Home and Community-Based Services	Data not available[b]	0	Data not available[b]
Medicaid State Plan Services	Data not available[b]	Data not available[b]	Data not available[b]
Money Follows the Person Rebalancing Demonstration	105,596,872	0	Data not available[b]
Department of Labor			
America's Heroes at Work	300,000	300,000	No response[i]
Disabled Veterans' Outreach Program	81,251,000	Data not available[b]	46,887
Employer Assistance and Resource Network	1,600,000	1,600,000	Not applicable (program serves employers)
Job Accommodation Network	2,366,318	2,366,318	12,800[j]
Job Corps[k]	1,712,000,000	Data not available[b]	12,079
Local Veterans' Employment Representatives program	76,481,000	Data not available[b]	36,322
REALifelines Initiative	Data not available[b]	Data not available[b]	9,376[l]
Registered Apprenticeship for Youth and Young Adults with Disabilities Initiative	0[m]	0	21[n]
Community Service Employment for Older Americans/Senior Community Service Employment Program[o]	825,400,000	Data not available[b]	17,885[p]
Veterans' Workforce Investment Program[q]	9,493,707	Data not available[b]	669[r]
Work Opportunity Tax Credit (joint with the Internal Revenue Service)	18,520,000[s]	0	33,644[t]
Workforce Investment Act Youth Activities	910,207,965	Data not available[b]	15,105[u]
Workforce Recruitment Program (joint with the Department of Defense)	211,377	211,377	2,157
YouthBuild[v]	97,375,000	Data not available[b]	425[r]
Department of Veterans Affairs			
Compensated Work Therapy program	0	0	30,000
Disabled Transition Assistance Program	Data not available[b]	Data not available[b]	36,386
Vocational Rehabilitation and Employment	768,000,000	768,000,000	94,912
Vocational Training and Rehabilitation for Vietnam Veterans' Children with Spina Bifida or Other Covered Birth Defects	Data not available[b]	Data not available[b]	14
Social Security Administration			
Work Incentives Planning and Assistance program[w]	27,328,266	27,328,266	51,395[x]

Program	Fiscal year 2010 obligation	Portion of fiscal year 2010 obligation for employment-related services and support for people with disabilities[a]	Number of people with disabilities provided employment services, fiscal year 2010
State Vocational Rehabilitation Cost Reimbursement Program	106,000,000	106,000,000	7,768[y]
Ticket to Work program	22,100,000[z]	22,100,000	55,093

Source: GAO survey.

[a]Some programs were not able to identify obligations related to providing employment supports to people with disabilities.

[b]"Data not available" indicates that the program was not able to provide data on obligations or the number of people with disabilities served. For example, some programs—like Labor's Workforce Investment Act Youth and YouthBuild programs—reported that they are not required to track the portion of obligations for employment-related services and support for people with disabilities.

[c]A significant portion of these obligations ($578,500,000) was for constructing healing campuses for wounded, ill, and injured soldiers.

[d]Data are from December 2010 to September 2011.

[e]Data are from June to October 2010.

[f]Data are from October to December 2010.

[g]This program was proposed to be consolidated or eliminated in Education's fiscal year 2012 budget request, but the department reported that funds were appropriated in fiscal year 2012. The program was also proposed to be consolidated or eliminated in Education's fiscal year 2013 budget request. In addition, Education officials noted that the Supported Employment Services program provides supplemental funding to help state VR agencies cover the costs of Supported Employment State Grants participating in the State Vocational Rehabilitation Services program.

[h]According to Education officials, there is no federal appropriation for this program. Direct federal costs to administer this program, including the costs of arbitrations, are covered by the Rehabilitation Services Administration's salaries and expenses budget. Costs at the state level are paid from various sources, including vocational rehabilitation formula grant funds (the state VR agency serving individuals who are blind administers the program), state funds, program income and set-aside funds from vendor income. Exact funding mechanisms vary by state.

[i]"No response" indicates that the program did not respond to this survey question or otherwise provide this information.

[j]Data are from September 2009 to September 2010. According to Labor, people with disabilities account for only about one third of the 36,500 individuals who contacted JAN for services. In addition, officials reported JAN receives 3.1 million Web page requests annually.

[k]Total program obligations for Job Corps includes $102 million in American Recovery and Reinvestment Act obligations. Data on participants is from program year 2009, and is based on self-disclosed and readily observable disabilities.

[l]Data are from May 2008 to October 2010. This data includes the number of participants contacted and services provided, including to spouses and caregivers.

[m]According to Labor, this program did not receive funds in fiscal year 2010 and continued operating on previous year's funding.

[n]Data are from June 2010 to June 2011.

[o]This program was proposed to be transferred to the Department of Health and Human Services in Labor's fiscal year 2013 budget request.

[p]Data are from July 2010 to June 2011.

[q]This program was proposed to be consolidated or eliminated in Labor's fiscal year 2013 budget request.

[r]Data are from July 2009 to June 2010.

[s]Reported obligations for the Work Opportunity Tax Credit are for Labor's administration of the program, according to agency officials. According to the Internal Revenue Service, in tax year 2009—the most recent data available—there were more than $600 million in Work Opportunity Tax Credits that were eligible to be claimed by individuals. In addition, for tax year 2009, there were more than $1 billion in Work Opportunity Tax Credits that were eligible to be claimed by corporations (including S corporations).

[t]According to Labor, this number represents certifications issued by State Workforce Agencies to employers that an employee has met the eligibility requirements for a Work Opportunity Tax Credit target group for individuals with disabilities.

[u]Data are from April 2009 to March 2010.

[v]Program reported appropriated funds instead of obligations.

[w]According to program officials, this program is expected to end by the end of fiscal year 2012.

[x]According to SSA officials, this number only indicates those enrolled and served in fiscal year 2010 and not those enrolled in a previous year and served in fiscal year 2010.

[y]This number represents the number of people who achieved the outcome of 9 months of working and earning at the substantial gainful activity level. As of October 25, 2010, the State Vocational Rehabilitation Cost Reimbursement Program had served 235,346 people. In addition, an SSA official noted that these participants may also be counted as participants in Education's State Vocational Rehabilitation Services program.

[z]Obligations reported for the Ticket to Work program in fiscal year 2010 represent the cost of funding the Employment Networks and not the total cost of the program. Data on total obligations for fiscal year 2010 will be available later in fiscal year 2012.

Appendix IV: Reported Program Objectives and Eligibility Requirements

Program title	Program objectives	Beneficiary eligibility requirements
U.S. AbilityOne Commission		
AbilityOne Program	The purpose of the Javits-Wagner-O'Day Act is to generate employment and training opportunities for people who are blind or have other severe disabilities in the manufacture and delivery of products and services to the federal government. The law requires federal agencies to procure certain products and services that are produced and provided by community-based nonprofit agencies that are dedicated to training and employing persons who are blind or have other severe disabilities.	The primary requirement for a nonprofit agency to participate in the AbilityOne Program is that, on an annual basis, 75 percent of all of the direct labor done at a nonprofit agency be performed by people who are blind or severely disabled. The term "blind" refers to an individual or class of individuals whose central visual acuity does not exceed 20/200 in the better eye with correcting lenses or whose visual acuity, if better than 20/200, is accompanied by a limit to the field of vision in the better eye to such a degree that its widest diameter subtends an angle of no greater than 20 degrees. The term "severely disabled" refers to an individual or class of individuals who has a severe physical or mental impairment other than blindness, which so limits the person's functional capabilities (mobility, communication, self-care, self direction, work tolerance, or work skills) that the individual is unable to engage in normal competitive employment, over an extended period of time.
Department of Agriculture		
Assistive Technology Program for Farmers with Disabilities: AgrAbility Project	AgrAbility increases the likelihood that individuals with disabilities and their families engaged in production agriculture (AgrAbility's customers) become more successful. The program supports cooperative projects in which State Cooperative Extension Services based at either 1862 or 1890 Land-Grant Universities or the University of the District of Columbia subcontract to private, nonprofit disability organizations. Measures of success may include improvements in customers' financial stability or access to life activities and in the capacity of the states and regions to deliver services this population requires in a timely and satisfying manner. To address the specialized needs of AgrAbility's customers, the program builds service capacity on national, regional, state, and local levels through education and networking. In the absence of capacity, projects provide assistance to customers. The primary function of the National AgrAbility Project is to support the state and regional projects in developing their capacity to meet these objectives.	The program targets accommodating disability in production agriculture. It provides education and awareness to the public, agricultural, and rehabilitation professionals on what can be done to accommodate disability in the agricultural workplace. The program does not fund rehabilitation equipment or payments to individuals.

Program title	Program objectives	Beneficiary eligibility requirements
Department of Defense		
Air Force Warrior and Survivor Care	Develop programs to help identify all airmen that need assistance; continue to build mentorship program to aid and benefit recovering airmen; employ dedicated qualified staff as Recovery Care Coordinators and provide them with tools and support needed to be successful; provide comprehensive policy for Mortuary, Casualty Affairs, Wounded Warrior, and Recovery Care Coordinator programs.	The Air Force Warrior and Survivor Care programs are made available to all Active Duty, Air National Guard, and Air Force Reserve members and their families to provide support in the event an airman is seriously wounded, ill, or injured while serving. The level of support and benefit assistance provided is dependent solely on need and is provided throughout the continuum of care. If injuries or illness warrant, airmen may enter the program at any time by self-referral or be referred by commander, spouses, supervisors, and medical personnel.
Army Warrior Care and Transition Program	An Army-wide structure to provide support and services for wounded, ill, and injured soldiers. The program enables the Army to evaluate and treat soldiers through a comprehensive, soldier-centric process of medical care, rehabilitation, professional development, and achievement of personal goals.	The Warrior Care and Transition Program is available to soldiers of all components (active and reserve components/active guard and reserve) on active duty who require complex medical care management of 6 months or longer duration. Additionally, eligibility is extended to activated reserve component soldiers requiring definitive medical care who have been approved by a Medical Review Board.
Computer/ Electronic Accommodations Program	The Computer/Electronic Accommodations Program (CAP) is a program in the TRICARE Management Activity, under the direction of the Assistant Secretary of Defense for Health Affairs. CAP's mission is to provide assistive technology and accommodation services to federal employees with disabilities and wounded servicemembers to increase access to information environment and employment opportunities in the federal government.	To be eligible for CAP services, an individual must be a federal employee with a disability in the Department of Defense or an employee with a disability at one of the federal partners with CAP or an active duty wounded or ill servicemember.
Marine Corps Wounded Warrior Regiment	To maintain a high level of coordination through a single command structure that delivers or facilitates delivery of nonmedical care to wounded, ill, or injured Marines and their families.	Must be an active duty, reserve, retired, or veteran wounded, ill, or injured Marine.
Marine Corps Wounded Warrior Intern Program	To provide job skills and training to wounded, ill, and injured Marines pending medical separation.	The Marine Corps Wounded Warrior Intern Program is open to all wounded, ill, and injured Marines. Spouses and caregivers of active duty wounded, ill, and injured Marines are eligible for some of the program benefits.

Program title	Program objectives	Beneficiary eligibility requirements
Navy Safe Harbor Program	1. Provide optimal nonmedical care to all Safe Harbor enrollees and their families throughout recovery, rehabilitation and reintegration 2. Cultivate and institutionalize external and internal partnerships 3. Provide focused outreach opportunities for wounded, ill, or injured sailors' and Coast Guardsmen's family members, caregivers and their support network 4. Increase awareness of Navy Safe Harbor 5. Align resources to effectively and efficiently execute the Safe Harbor mission 6. Attract and retain sustained superior performers with demonstrated leadership expertise to the Safe Harbor staff.	All seriously wounded, ill, or injured sailors and Coast Guardsmen not likely to return to duty in 180 days and likely to be medically retired or separated; and high-risk, nonseriously wounded, ill, or injured sailors, Coast Guardsmen and their families (case-by-case).
Recovery Care Coordinator Program	The Recovery Care Coordinators (RCC) assist in the creation and management of the Comprehensive Recovery Plans for Wounded Warriors—Army, Marines, Navy, Air Force, and U.S. Special Operations Command—until they are either returned to duty or separated from the service due to the extent of their injuries. The RCCs act as the single point of contact for the Wounded Warriors and their families as they receive care from multi-disciplinary support teams, both medical and nonmedical, in helping them obtain required treatment, care, and family assistance.	Populations served by the RCCs are wounded, ill and injured warriors and their families: troop program unit, Active Guard Reserve, Individual Mobilization Augmentee, Individual Ready Reserve, retirees, and veterans.

Program title	Program objectives	Beneficiary eligibility requirements
Recovery Coordination Program-Operation Warfighter (internships)	Operation Warfighter (OWF) is a federal internship program for wounded, ill, and injured servicemembers. The main objective of OWF is to place servicemembers in supportive work settings that positively impact their recuperation. The program represents a great opportunity for transitioning servicemembers to augment their employment readiness by building their resumes, exploring employment interests, developing job skills, benefiting from both formal and on-the-job training opportunities, and gaining valuable federal government work experience that will help prepare them for the future. Operation Warfighter strives to demonstrate to participants that the skills they have obtained in the military are transferable into civilian employment. For servicemembers returning to duty, the program enables these participants to maintain their skill sets and provides the opportunity for additional training and experience that can subsequently benefit the military. Operation Warfighter simultaneously enables federal employers to better familiarize themselves with the skill sets and challenges of wounded, ill, and injured servicemembers as well as benefit from the considerable talent and dedication of these servicemembers.	Eligibility criteria require participants to be servicemembers in an active duty status assigned to a military treatment facility or a service wounded warrior program. If not assigned to one of these programs, servicemembers can still be eligible if they are going through the medical evaluation board and their chain of command approves their participation.
U.S. Special Operations Command Care Coalition	To provide Special Operations Forces warriors and their families a model advocacy program in order to enhance their quality of life and strengthen overall readiness of Special Operations.	Special Operations Forces wounded, ill, or injured servicemembers and their families
Department of Education		
American Indian Vocational Rehabilitation Services	To provide vocational rehabilitation services to American Indians with disabilities who reside on or near federal or state reservations in order to achieve gainful employment.	American Indians with disabilities residing on or near a federal or state reservation (including Native Alaskans) who meet the definition of an individual with a disability in Section 7 (8)(A) of the Rehabilitation Act.
Assistive Technology State Grant program	To provide states with financial assistance that supports programs designed to maximize the ability of individuals of all ages with disabilities and their family members, guardians, advocates, and authorized representatives to obtain assistive technology devices and assistive technology services.	Individuals with disabilities.

Program title	Program objectives	Beneficiary eligibility requirements
Helen Keller National Center for Deaf-Blind Youths and Adults	Authorized by an Act of Congress in 1967, the Helen Keller National Center for Deaf-Blind Youths and Adults is a national rehabilitation program serving youth and adults who are deaf-blind. The purposes of the Center are to (1) provide specialized intensive services, or any other services, at the Center or anywhere else in the United States, which are necessary to encourage the maximum personal development of any individual who is deaf-blind; (2) train family members of individuals who are deaf-blind at the Center or anywhere else in the United States, in order to assist family members in providing and obtaining appropriate services for the individual who is deaf-blind; (3) train professionals and allied personnel at the Center or anywhere else in the United States to provide services to individuals who are deaf-blind; and (4) conduct applied research, development programs, and demonstrations with respect to communication techniques, teaching methods, aids and devices, and delivery of services.	The Helen Keller National Center for Deaf-Blind Youths and Adults provides services on a national basis to adults who are deaf-blind, their families, and service providers. The term "individual who is deaf-blind" means any individual - (A)(i) who has a central visual acuity of 20/200 or less in the better eye with corrective lenses, or a field defect such that the peripheral diameter of visual field subtends an angular distance no greater than 20 degrees, or a progressive visual loss having a prognosis leading to one or both these conditions; (ii) who has a chronic hearing impairment so severe that most speech cannot be understood with optimum amplification, or a progressive hearing loss having a prognosis leading to this condition; and (iii) for whom the combination of impairments described in clauses (i) and (ii) cause extreme difficulty in attaining independence in daily life activities, achieving psychosocial adjustment, or obtaining a vocation; (B) who despite the inability to be measured accurately for hearing and vision loss due to cognitive or behavioral constraints, or both, can be determined through functional and performance assessment to have severe hearing and visual disabilities that cause extreme difficulty in attaining independence in daily life activities, achieving psychosocial adjustment, or obtaining vocational objectives; or (C) meets such other requirements as the Secretary may prescribe by regulation."
Migrant and Seasonal Farmworkers	The Migrant and Seasonal Farmworkers program provides comprehensive vocational rehabilitation (VR) services available to migrant and seasonal farmworkers with disabilities with the goal of increasing employment opportunities for these individuals. Projects also develop innovative methods for reaching and serving this population. Projects are required to coordinate with the VR State Grants program.	Individuals with disabilities and individuals with significant disabilities as defined in Sections 7(9)(A)(B) and 7(20)(A), respectively, of the Rehabilitation Act of 1973, as amended.
Model Comprehensive Transition and Postsecondary Programs for Students with Intellectual Disabilities	Create or expand model comprehensive transition and postsecondary programs for students with intellectual disabilities. Funds also support a coordinating center that provides related services.	Students with intellectual disabilities enrolled in model programs or other comprehensive transition and postsecondary programs.

Program title	Program objectives	Beneficiary eligibility requirements
Randolph-Sheppard Vending Facility Program	According to the statute creating the Randolph-Sheppard program, the objectives of this initiative include providing blind persons with remunerative employment, enlarging the economic opportunities of the blind, and stimulating the blind to greater efforts in striving to make themselves self-supporting. Toward this end, blind persons licensed under the provisions of this chapter shall be authorized to operate vending facilities on any federal property. In layman language, the program's objectives are to create employment opportunities by creating a priority for eligible blind people to operate entrepreneurial ventures on federal and other designated state properties. Throughout the country, states have created similar priorities to mirror the federal program in their specific jurisdictions.	To be eligible for this program, participants must be blind, citizens of the United States, and meet any other specific standards that individual state licensing agencies may require.
Rehabilitation Services Demonstration and Training Programs	To provide financial assistance to projects and demonstrations for expanding and improving the provision of rehabilitation and other services authorized under the Rehabilitation Act, or that further the purposes of the act, including related research and evaluation activities.	Individuals with disabilities.[a]
State Vocational Rehabilitation Services	To assist states in operating comprehensive, coordinated, effective, efficient, and accountable programs of vocational rehabilitation; to assess, plan, develop, and provide vocational rehabilitation services for individuals with disabilities, consistent with their strengths, resources, priorities, concerns, abilities, and capabilities so they may prepare for and engage in competitive employment.	Eligibility for vocational rehabilitation services is based on the presence of a physical or mental impairment, which for such an individual constitutes or results in a substantial impediment to employment, and the need for vocational rehabilitation services that may be expected to benefit the individual in terms of an employment outcome.
Supported Employment State Grants	To provide grants for time-limited services leading to supported employment for individuals with the most severe disabilities to enable such individuals to achieve the employment outcome of supported employment.	Individuals with the most severe disabilities whose ability or potential to engage in a training program leading to supported employment has been determined by evaluating rehabilitation potential. In addition, individuals must need extended services in order to perform competitive work and have the ability to work in a supported employment setting.
Department of Health and Human Services		
1915(c) Home and Community-Based Services Waiver	The Medicaid Home and Community-based Services waiver program is authorized in section 1915(c) of the Social Security Act. The program permits a state to furnish an array of home and community based services that assist Medicaid beneficiaries to live in the community and avoid institutionalization.	In order to participate in a waiver, a person must meet the level of care specified for the waiver and also be a member of a Medicaid eligibility group that a state includes in the waiver. A state may include a Medicaid eligibility group in the waiver only when it includes the same group in its state plan.

Program title	Program objectives	Beneficiary eligibility requirements
1915(i) State Plan Home and Community-Based Services	1915(i) allows states the option to add home and community-based services to their Medicaid State Plans.	Financial eligibility requirements: (1) eligible for Medicaid and have income up to 150 percent of the federal poverty level, and (2) at the state's option, eligible through a new Medicaid eligibility category at income up to 300 percent of Supplemental Security Income Federal Benefit Rate and eligible for a 1915(c) waiver or 1115 demonstration program in their state. Other eligibility requirements: (1) meet state-defined needs-based criteria, and (2) at the state's option, meet the state-specified targeted population group for the 1915(i) benefit.
Medicaid State Plan Services	To provide parameters for the coverage of services authorized by the Social Security Act to be part of the Medicaid State Plan.	Each state plan service contains, either in statute or regulation, parameters for service provision, including any functional eligibility requirements to be met.
Money Follows the Person Rebalancing Demonstration	The Money Follows the Person (MFP) Rebalancing Demonstration, authorized by section 6071 of the Deficit Reduction Act of 2005 (Pub. Law No.109-171), was designed to assist States to balance their long-term care systems and help Medicaid enrollees transition from institutions to the community. Congress initially authorized up to $1.75 billion in funds through federal fiscal year 2011. With the subsequent passage of the Patient Protection and Affordable Care Act (Pub. Law No.111-148) in 2010, Section 2403 extended the program through September 30, 2016. An additional $2.25 billion in federal funds was appropriated through federal fiscal year 2016. The MFP Demonstration supports state efforts to rebalance their long-term support system so that individuals have a choice of where they live and receive services. Transition individuals from institutions who want to live in the community.	As defined in Section 6071(b)(2) of the DRA and amended by Section 2403 of the Affordable Care Act, the term "eligible individual" means an individual in the state who, immediately before beginning participation in the MFP demonstration project: (1) resides (and has resided, for a period of not less than 90 consecutive days) in a qualified institution or inpatient setting (excluding days solely for the purpose of short-term rehabilitation services); (2) is receiving Medicaid benefits for services furnished by such qualified institution or inpatient setting; and (3) with respect to whom a determination has been made that, but for the provision of home and community-based long-term care services, the individual would continue to require the level of care provided in a qualified institution or inpatient setting.
Department of Labor		
America's Heroes at Work	America's Heroes at Work is a Department of Labor project that addresses the employment challenges of returning servicemembers living with Traumatic Brain Injury (TBI) or Post-Traumatic Stress Disorder (PTSD)—an important focus of the President's veterans agenda. The project equips employers and the workforce development system with the tools they need to help returning servicemembers affected by TBI and/or PTSD succeed in the workplace—particularly servicemembers returning from Iraq and Afghanistan.	No eligibility requirements. Support services (website, toll-free assistance, and presentations) are available to any group or individual that requests them.

Program title	Program objectives	Beneficiary eligibility requirements
Community Service Employment for Older Americans/Senior Community Service Employment Program	The purpose of the Senior Community Service Employment Program (SCSEP) program is to provide, foster, and promote useful part-time work opportunities (usually 20 hours per week) in community service training and employment activities for unemployed low-income persons who are 55 years of age and older. To the extent feasible, SCSEP assists and promotes the transition of program participants into unsubsidized employment.	Unemployed persons 55 years or older whose family is low-income (i.e., income does not exceed the low-income standards defined in 20 CFR section 641.507) are eligible for enrollment (20 CFR section 641.500). Low-income means an income of the family which, during the preceding 6 months on an annualized basis or the actual income during the preceding 12 months, at the option of the grantee, is not more than 125 percent of the poverty levels established and periodically updated by the Department of Health and Human Services (42 USC 3056p(a)(4)). The poverty guidelines are issued each year in the Federal Register and the Department of Health and Human Services maintains a page on the Internet which provides the poverty guidelines (http://www.aspe.hhs.gov/poverty/index.shtml, accessed May 30, 2012). Enrollee eligibility is re-determined on an annual basis (20 CFR section 641.505).
Disabled Veterans' Outreach Program	To provide intensive services to meet the employment needs of disabled and other eligible veterans with maximum emphasis in meeting the employment needs of those who are economically or educationally disadvantaged, including homeless veterans and veterans with barriers to employment.	Eligible veterans and eligible persons with emphasis on Special Disabled veterans, disabled veterans, economically or educationally disadvantaged veterans, and veterans with other barriers to employment.
Employer Assistance and Resource Network (EARN)	EARN is a resource for employers seeking to recruit, retain and advance individuals with disabilities. (www.askearn.org, accessed May 30, 2012)	Any public or private employer seeking to advance the employment of individuals with disabilities is eligible for services.
Job Accommodation Network (JAN)	The mission of JAN is to facilitate the employment and retention of workers with disabilities by providing employers, employment providers, people with disabilities, their family members, and other interested parties with technical assistance on job accommodations, entrepreneurship, and related subjects. JAN's efforts are in support of the employment, including self-employment and small business ownership, of people with disabilities. This free, confidential technical assistance is provided in English and Spanish via telephone, email, chat, and postal mail.	JAN services are available to all interested parties.

GAO-12-677 Employment for People with Disabilities

Program title	Program objectives	Beneficiary eligibility requirements
Job Corps	Job Corps is the nation's largest federally funded training program that provides at-risk youth, ages 16-24, with academic instruction, toward the achievement of a High School Diploma or General Education Development (GED) certificate, and career training in high-growth, high-demand industries. Upon exit from the program, participants receive transition assistance to employment, higher education, or the military. The program is primarily residential, serving nearly 60,000 students at 125 centers nationwide.	To be eligible to become an enrollee, an individual shall be: (1) not less than age 16 and not more than age 21 on the date of enrollment, except that (a) not more than 20 percent of the individuals enrolled in the Job Corps may be not less than age 22 and not more than age 24 on the date of enrollment, and (b) either such maximum age limitation may be waived by the Secretary, in accordance with regulations of the Secretary, in the case of an individual with a disability; (2) a low-income individual; and (3) an individual who is one or more of the following: (a) basic skills deficient; (b) a school dropout; (c) homeless, a runaway, or a foster child; (d) a parent; (e) an individual who requires additional education, vocational training, or intensive counseling and related assistance, in order to participate successfully in regular schoolwork or to secure and hold employment.
Local Veterans' Employment Representatives program	Conduct outreach and provide seminars to employers which advocates hiring of veterans; facilitate Transition Assistance Program employment workshops to transitioning servicemembers; establish and conduct job search workshops; facilitate employment, training, and placement services furnished to veterans in a state under the applicable state employment service or one-stop career center delivery systems whose sole purpose is to assist veterans in gaining and retaining employment.	Eligible veterans and eligible persons.
REALifelines Initiative	The objective of REALifelines is to support the economic recovery of transitioning servicemembers and veterans who were wounded or injured while serving in Operation Iraqi Freedom or Operation Enduring Freedom. The transition services are extended to spouses and caregivers through the resources at the one-stop career centers. Intensive services are provided by our Disabled Veterans Outreach Program specialists. The specialized services are intended to identify and address any barriers to employment.	Transitioning servicemembers and veterans who were wounded or injured while serving in Operation Iraqi Freedom or Operation Enduring Freedom.
Registered Apprenticeship for Youth and Young Adults with Disabilities Initiative	Increases systems capacity for integrated, inclusive apprenticeship training for youth and young adults with a full range of disabilities	Youth and young adults with disabilities ages 16 through 27.
Veterans' Workforce Investment Program	To provide services to assist in reintegrating eligible veterans into meaningful employment within the labor force and to stimulate the development of effective service delivery systems that will address the complex problems facing eligible veterans.	Service-connected disabled veterans, veterans who have significant barriers to employment, veterans who served on active duty in the armed forces during a war or in a campaign or expedition for which a campaign badge has been authorized, and veterans who are recently separated from military service (48 months).

Program title	Program objectives	Beneficiary eligibility requirements
Workforce Investment Act Youth Activities	To help low-income youth, between the ages of 14 and 21, acquire the educational and occupational skills, training, and support needed to achieve academic and employment success and successfully transition to careers and productive adulthood.	An eligible youth is an individual who: (1) is 14 to 21 years of age; (2) is an individual who received an income or is a member of a family that received a total family income that, in relation to family size, does not exceed the higher of (a) the poverty line or (b) 70 percent of the lower living standard income; and (3) meets one or more of the following criteria: is an individual who is deficient in basic literacy skills, a school dropout, homeless, a runaway, a foster child, pregnant or a parent, an offender, or requires additional assistance to complete their education or secure and hold employment.

There is an exception to permit youth who are not low-income individuals to receive youth services. Up to 5 percent of youth participants served by youth programs in a local area may be individuals who do not meet the income criterion for eligible youth, provided that they are within one or more of the following categories: school dropout; basic skills deficient; are one or more grade levels below the grade level appropriate to the individual's age; pregnant or parenting; possess one or more disabilities, including learn disabilities; homeless or runaway; offender; or face serious barriers to employment as identified by the local board. |
| Work Opportunity Tax Credit (joint with the Internal Revenue Service) | The tax credit was designed to help individuals from 12 target groups who consistently have faced significant barriers to employment move from economic dependency to self-sufficiency by encouraging businesses in the private sector to hire target group members and be eligible to claim tax credits based on the wages they paid to the new hires during the first year of employment, up to a dollar wage limit. | All employers seeking Work Opportunity Tax Credit target group workers and target group members seeking employment. The members of the different target groups have statutory definitions (per Pub. Law No. 109-188, as amended) with specific eligibility requirements that must be verified by the state workforce agencies before a certification can be issued to an employer or his representatives. Participating employers and their representatives must file their certification requests using Internal Revenue Service Form 8850 and ETA Form 9061 or 9062 within 28 days after the employment-start day of the new hires. This timeliness requirement cannot be waived and must be met before a state can issue a certification for eligible target group members. |
| Workforce Recruitment Program (joint with the Department of Defense) | The Workforce Recruitment Program is a recruitment and referral program that connects federal and private sector employers nationwide with highly motivated postsecondary students and recent graduates with disabilities who are eager to prove their abilities in the workplace through summer or permanent jobs. | The Workforce Recruitment Program for College Students with Disabilities serves individuals who have disabilities, are enrolled at an accredited institution of higher learning on a substantially full-time basis (unless the severity of the disability precludes the student from taking a substantially full-time load) to seek a degree or are enrolled at such an institution as a degree-seeking student taking less than a substantially full-time load in the enrollment period immediately prior to graduation or have graduated with a degree from such an institution within the past year, and are U.S. citizens. |

Program title	Program objectives	Beneficiary eligibility requirements
YouthBuild	Provides disadvantaged youth with education and employment skills necessary to achieve economic self sufficiency in high demand occupations	Youth ages 16 through 24 and a member of a disadvantaged population, such as: low-income, foster care (including youth aging out of foster care), youth offender, youth with a disability, child of an incarcerated parent, high school dropout, or migrant youth.

Department of Veterans Affairs

Compensated Work Therapy program	Compensated Work Therapy is a recovery-oriented, vocational model integrated into the continuum of Veterans Health Administration's services, as authorized by 38 USC § 1718. Department of Veterans Affairs (VA) medical centers offer Compensated Work Therapy with both Transitional Work Experience and Supported Employment services for veterans with occupational dysfunctions resulting from their mental health conditions, or who are unsuccessful at obtaining or maintaining stable employment patterns due to mental illnesses or physical impairments co-occurring with mental illnesses. The scope of Therapeutic and Supported Employment Services (TSES) includes skill development opportunities both for veterans for whom the primary objective is competitive employment, and for veterans in need of therapeutic pre-employment services designed to ameliorate the consequences of long standing mental health problems alone or with co-occurring physical illness. The mission of TSES is to improve the veteran's overall quality of life through a vocational rehabilitation experience in which the veteran learns new job skills, strengthen successful work habits, and regains a sense of self-esteem and self-worth. The vision of TSES is that all veterans challenged with physical or mental illness can obtain meaningful competitive employment in the community, working in jobs of their choice, while receiving necessary and appropriate support services. The goal of TSES is to provide a continuum of therapeutic and skill development services for veterans who have difficulty obtaining or maintaining stable employment patterns due to mental illnesses or physical impairments co-occurring with mental illnesses. The objectives of TSES are to provide an opportunity for work hardening and skill development services to eligible veterans regardless of diagnosis, disability, or treatment goals; Collaborate with veterans and their primary treatment team to assure each veteran has the support necessary to achieve his or her vocational goals; Ensure access to all components in the continuum of TSES services as the veteran's needs change over the course of treatment, rehabilitation, and recovery.	A person who served in the active military, naval, or air service and who was discharged or released under conditions other than dishonorable may qualify for VA health care benefits. Reservists and National Guard members may also qualify for VA health care benefits if they were called to active duty (other than for training only) by a federal order and completed the full period for which they were called or ordered to active duty.

Program title	Program objectives	Beneficiary eligibility requirements
Disabled Transition Assistance Program (DTAP)	DTAP is an integral component of transition assistance that involves intervening on behalf of servicemembers who may be released because of a disability or who believe they have a disability qualifying them for VA's Vocational Rehabilitation and Employment program (VR&E). The goal of DTAP is to encourage and assist potentially eligible servicemembers in making an informed decision about VA's VR&E program. It is also intended to facilitate the expeditious delivery of vocational rehabilitation services to eligible persons by assisting them in filing an application for vocational rehabilitation benefits.	Servicemembers who may be released because of injuries or diseases that happened while on active duty, or were made worse by active military service.
Vocational Rehabilitation and Employment (VR&E)	To provide all services and assistance necessary to enable service-disabled veterans and service persons hospitalized or receiving outpatient medical care services or treatment for a service-connected disability pending discharge to gain and maintain suitable employment. When employment is not reasonably feasible, the program can provide the needed services and assistance to help the individual achieve maximum independence in daily living. The VR&E program is a comprehensive vocational rehabilitation program that provides up to 48 months of extensive services leading to employment. Every VR&E program participant is provided a comprehensive vocational evaluation to determine transferable skills, aptitudes, and interests; explore labor market and wage information; and to focus on vocational options that will lead to a viable suitable employment or independent living goal. Results from the evaluation help determine which of the five tracks to success (Reemployment, Rapid Access to Employment, Self Employment, Employment Through Long-term Services, or Independent Living) is most appropriate. Depending on the rehabilitation needs of the individual, services may include training such as on-the-job, vocational/technical school, college-level (certificate, 2-year degree, 4-year degree, or beyond). VR&E pays for tuition, fees, books, and supplies associated with training, as well as a monthly subsistence allowance.	Veterans of World War II and later service with a service-connected disability or disabilities rated at least 20 percent compensable and certain service-disabled servicepersons pending discharge or release from service if VA determines the servicepersons will likely receive at least a 20 percent rating and they need vocational rehabilitation because of an employment handicap. Veterans with compensable ratings of 10 percent may also be eligible if they are found to have a serious employment handicap. To receive an evaluation for vocational rehabilitation services, a veteran must have received, or eventually receive, an honorable or other than dishonorable discharge, have a VA service-connected disability rating of 10 percent or more, and apply for vocational rehabilitation services.

Program title	Program objectives	Beneficiary eligibility requirements
Vocational Training and Rehabilitation for Vietnam Veterans' Children with Spina Bifida or Other Covered Birth Defects	To provide vocational training and rehabilitation to certain children born with spina bifida or other covered birth defects who are children of Vietnam veterans and some Korean veterans.	A child born with spina bifida or other covered birth defects, except spina bifida occulta, who is the natural child of a Vietnam veteran and some Korean veterans, regardless of the age or marital status of the child, conceived after the date on which the veteran first served in the Republic of Vietnam during the Vietnam era and in particular areas near the demilitarized zone (DMZ) in the Korean conflict. VA must also determine that it is feasible for the child to achieve a vocational goal.
Social Security Administration		
Work Incentives Planning and Assistance program	To comply with the Ticket to Work and Work Incentives Improvement Act which was passed in December 1999, and reauthorized by the Social Security Protection Act of 2004, which requires SSA to establish a community based work incentives planning and assistance program. The purpose of this program is to disseminate accurate information to SSA disability beneficiaries (including transition to work aged youth) about work incentives programs, and issues related to such programs, to enable them to make informed choices about working and whether or when to assign their Ticket to Work, as well as how available work incentives can facilitate their transition into the workforce. The ultimate goal of the Work Incentives Planning and Assistance program is to assist SSA disability beneficiaries succeed in their return to work efforts.	All individuals within the state who are entitled to Social Security Disability Insurance benefits or eligible for Supplemental Security Income payments based on disability or blindness.
State Vocational Rehabilitation Cost Reimbursement Program	Makes vocational rehabilitation services more readily available to disabled or blind SSA disability beneficiaries.	Social Security Disability Insurance beneficiaries and Supplemental Security Income disability recipients
Ticket to Work program	Provides SSA disability beneficiaries more choices for receiving employment services.	Social Security Disability Insurance beneficiaries and Supplemental Security Income disability recipients ages 18 through 64.

Source: GAO survey.

[a]In commenting on a draft of this report, Education noted that Rehabilitation Services Demonstration and Training Programs grantees may use funds to conduct a broad range of activities, the ultimate goal of which is to improve services for individuals with disabilities. However, in some cases, individuals with disabilities may not be the direct target population. For example, some of the program funds are used for providing training and technical assistance to service providers and parents of individuals with disabilities.

Appendix V: Services Reported to Be Provided in Fiscal Year 2010, by Population and Program

Table 5: Services Provided by 19 Programs That Limit Eligibility to Servicemembers, Veterans, and/or Their Families

	Employment counseling, assessment, and case management	Assistance in earning a high school diploma or its equivalent	Job development	Job readiness skills	Job recruitment and referrals	Job retention training	Job search or job placement activities	Occupational or vocational training	Vocational rehabilitation	Supported employment	On-the-job training	Remedial academic, English language skills, or adult literacy	Work experience	Employment-related information dissemination	Entrepreneurship training and support	Tax expenditures related to workers with disabilities	Support and services to employers of people with disabilities	Assistive technology and workplace accommodations
Air Force Warrior and Survivor Care	●	●	●	●	●	●	●	○	○	○	○	●		○	*		●	●
America's Heroes at Work	○	○	○	*	*	○	*	○	○	*	○		*	●	*		●	●
Army Warrior Care and Transition Program	●	○	●	●	●	●	●	●	●	○	●	○	●	●			●	●
Compensated Work Therapy program	●		●	●	●	●	●	●	●	●	●	●	●	●		○	○	*
Computer/Electronic Accommodations Program	○			○		○					○		○	○			○	●
Disabled Transition Assistance Program	*	*	*	*	*	*	*	*	*	*	*	*	*	*	*		*	*
Disabled Veterans' Outreach Program	●	●	○	●	●	○	●						*	○	*		*	
Local Veterans' Employment Representatives program	○		●	●	○	○	●						*	●	*			

Table of employment-related services provided by various Department of Defense and Department of Labor/VA programs.

Service	Vocational Rehabilitation and Employment	Veterans' Workforce Investment Program	U.S. Special Operations Command Care Coalition	Recovery Care Coordinator Program	REALifelines Initiative	Operation Warfighter	Navy Safe Harbor Program	Marine Corps Wounded Warrior Regiment	Marine Corps Wounded Warrior Intern Program
Employment counseling, assessment, and case management	●	●			●	●	○	●	●
Assistance in earning a high school diploma or its equivalent	*	*							*
Job development	●	●			●	●	○	●	●
Job readiness skills	●	●	*		●	●	○	●	●
Job recruitment and referrals	●	●	*		●	*	○	●	●
Job retention training	●	○			●				*
Job search or job placement activities	●	●	*		●	*	○	●	●
Occupational or vocational training	●	●			○	●	○	○	●
Vocational rehabilitation	●				●	○	○	○	○
Supported employment	*				○	○	○	○	●
On-the-job training	●	○			*	●	○	○	●
Remedial academic, English language skills, or adult literacy	*				*				
Work experience	●	○				●	○		●
Employment-related information dissemination	●	○	*	○	●	○	○		●
Entrepreneurship training and support	●				●	○			*
Tax expenditures related to workers with disabilities									
Support and services to employers of people with disabilities	●				●	*	○	○	●
Assistive technology and workplace accommodations	●				●	○	○		○

Service	Vocational Training and Rehabilitation for Vietnam Veterans' Children with Spina Bifida or Other Covered Birth Defects	Work Opportunity Tax Credit
Employment counseling, assessment, and case management	●	
Assistance in earning a high school diploma or its equivalent	*	
Job development	●	
Job readiness skills	●	
Job recruitment and referrals	●	
Job retention training	●	
Job search or job placement activities	●	
Occupational or vocational training	●	
Vocational rehabilitation	●	
Supported employment		
On-the-job training		
Remedial academic, English language skills, or adult literacy	●	
Work experience		
Employment-related information dissemination		●
Entrepreneurship training and support		
Tax expenditures related to workers with disabilities		●
Support and services to employers of people with disabilities		○
Assistive technology and workplace accommodations	*	

Source: GAO survey.

● Service provided to more than 50 percent of program participants

○ Service provided to less than 50 percent of program participants

* Service provided, but extent unknown

Table 6: Services Provided by Five Programs That Limit Eligibility to Students, Transition Age Youth, and/or Young Adults

Service	Model Comprehensive Transition and Postsecondary Programs for Students with Intellectual Disabilities	Registered Apprenticeship Youth and Young Adults with Disabilities Initiative	Workforce Investment Act Youth Activities	Workforce Recruitment Program	YouthBuild
Employment counseling, assessment, and case management		○	●	*	●
Assistance in earning a high school diploma or its equivalent	*	*	*		●
Job development		*	*		●
Job readiness skills		*	*	*	●
Job recruitment and referrals		*	*	●	*
Job retention training		*	*		*
Job search or job placement activities		*	*	*	●
Occupational or vocational training		*	*		●
Vocational rehabilitation	*				
Supported employment			*		
On-the-job training		*	*		
Remedial academic, English language skills, or adult literacy		*	*		●
Work experience		*	*	●	●
Employment-related information dissemination		*	*	●	●
Entrepreneurship training and support		*	*		
Tax expenditures related to workers with disabilities					
Support and services to employers of people with disabilities		*		○	
Assistive technology and workplace accommodations		*	*	*	

Source: GAO survey.

● Service provided to more than 50 percent of program participants
○ Service provided to less than 50 percent of program participants
* Service provided, but extent unknown

Program	Employment counseling, assessment, and case management	Assistance in earning a high school diploma or its equivalent	Job development	Job readiness skills	Job recruitment and referrals	Job retention training	Job search or job placement activities	Occupational or vocational training	Vocational rehabilitation	Supported employment	On-the-job training	Remedial academic, English language skills, or adult literacy	Work experience	Employment-related information dissemination	Entrepreneurship training and support	Tax expenditures related to workers with disabilities	Support and services to employers of people with disabilities	Assistive technology and workplace accommodations
1915(i) State Plan Home and Community-Based Services	*		*	*	*	*	*	*	○	*	*			*				
Job Accommodation Network														●			●	●
Job Corps	●	●	●	●	●	●	●	●			●	●	●	●				
Medicaid State Plan Services	*			*						*								*
Rehabilitation Services Demonstration and Training Programs	*	*	*	*	*	*	*	*	*	*	*	*	*	*			*	*
Assistive Technology State Grant program															*			●
State Vocational Rehabilitation Services	●	○	○	○	○	○	●	●	●	○	○	○	○	●	○		○	○

Source: GAO survey.

● Service provided to more than 50 percent of program participants

○ Service provided to less than 50 percent of program participants

* Service provided, but extent unknown

Table 8: Services Provided by 14 Programs That Limit Eligibility to Other Populations

Program	Population served	Employment counseling, assessment, and case management	Assistance in earning a high school diploma or its equivalent	Job development	Job readiness skills	Job recruitment and referrals	Job retention training	Job search or job placement activities	Occupational or vocational training	Vocational rehabilitation	Supported employment	On-the-job training	Remedial academic, English language skills, or basic adult literacy	Work experience	Employment-related information dissemination	Entrepreneurship training and support	Tax expenditures	Support and services to employers of people with disabilities	Assistive technology and workplace accommodations
1915(c) Home and Community Based Services Waiver	Low-income persons	*		*	*	*	*	*			*	*			*	*			*
AbilityOne Program	People who are blind or visually impaired or have other significant disabilities																		
American Indian Vocational Rehabilitation Services	American Indians with disabilities	●	○	●	●	●	○	○	○	●	○	○	*	*	*	*		*	*
Assistive Technology Program for Farmers with Disabilities: AgrAbility Project	Profession-specific persons	●								*								*	*

Service	Community Service Employment for Older Americans/Senior Community Service Employment Program (Unemployed low-income persons 55 and older)	Employer Assistance and Resource Network (Employers of people with disabilities)	Helen Keller National Center for Deaf-Blind Youths and Adults (People who are deaf-blind)	Migrant and Seasonal Farmworkers (Other population groups)
Employment counseling, assessment, and case management	•		•	•
Assistance in earning a high school diploma or its equivalent				*
Job development	○		○	•
Job readiness skills	•		•	•
Job recruitment and referrals	•		○	•
Job retention training	•		•	•
Job search or job placement activities	•	○	•	•
Occupational or vocational training	○		•	•
Vocational rehabilitation	*		•	•
Supported employment	*		○	*
On-the-job training	*		•	•
Remedial academic, English language skills, or basic adult literacy	*			○
Work experience	•		○	
Employment-related information dissemination	•		•	○
Entrepreneurship training and support	*			
Tax expenditures				
Support and services to employers of people with disabilities	*	○	○	○
Assistive technology and workplace accommodations	○		*	○

Program	Population served	Employment counseling, assessment, and case management	Assistance in earning a high school diploma or its equivalent	Job development	Job readiness skills	Job recruitment and referrals	Job retention training	Job search or job placement activities	Occupational or vocational training	Vocational rehabilitation	Supported employment	On-the-job training	Remedial academic, English language skills, or basic adult literacy	Work experience	Employment-related information dissemination	Entrepreneurship training and support	Tax expenditures	Support and services to employers of people with disabilities	Assistive technology and workplace accommodations
Money Follows the Person Rebalancing Demonstration	People with other types of disabilities	*	*	*	*	*	*	*			*	*			*			*	*
Randolph-Sheppard Vending Facility Program	People who are blind	*	○	*	○	○	○	○	●	●		○		●	*	●		*	*
State Vocational Rehabilitation Cost Reimbursement Program	People who receive Supplemental Security Income or Social Security Disability Insurance benefits	●	○	○	○	○	○	●	○	●	○	○	*	○	○	○		○	○
Supported Employment State Grants	People with the most significant disabilities	●	○	●	●	○	○	●	○	●	●	○	○	●	○	○		○	○

Population served	Employment counseling, assessment, and case management	Assistance in earning a high school diploma or its equivalent	Job development	Job readiness skills	Job recruitment and referrals	Job retention training	Job search or job placement activities	Occupational or vocational training	Vocational rehabilitation	Supported employment	On-the-job training	Remedial academic, English language skills, or basic adult literacy	Work experience	Employment-related information dissemination	Entrepreneurship training and support	Tax expenditures	Support and services to employers of people with disabilities	Assistive technology and workplace accommodations
Ticket to Work program — People who receive Supplemental Security Income or Social Security Disability Insurance benefits	●	*	*	*	*	*	●	*	*	*	*		*	●	*		*	*
Work Incentives Planning and Assistance program — People who receive Supplemental Security Income or Social Security Disability Insurance benefits														●				

Source: GAO survey.

● Service provided to more than 50 percent of program participants

○ Service provided to less than 50 percent of program participants

* Service provided, but extent unknown

Appendix VI: Employment-Related Outcome Measures Programs Reported Tracking for People with Disabilities in Fiscal Year 2010

	Educational attainment	Credential attainment	Entered the military, postsecondary education, or vocational training program	Entered employment	Employment retention	Wage gain or change	Customer satisfaction	Reduced reliance on federal cash benefits	Other	Measures tracked specifically for people with disabilities
U.S. AbilityOne Commission										
AbilityOne Program				●		●	●		●	●
Department of Agriculture										
Assistive Technology Program for Farmers with Disabilities: AgrAbility Project										
Department of Defense										
Air Force Warrior and Survivor Care										
Army Warrior Care and Transition Program				●			●			
Computer/Electronic Accommodations Program					●		●			●
Marine Corps Wounded Warrior Intern Program				●						●
Marine Corps Wounded Warrior Regiment			●	●	●					●

	Educational attainment	Credential attainment	Entered the military, postsecondary education, or vocational training program	Entered employment	Employment retention	Wage gain or change	Customer satisfaction	Reduced reliance on federal cash benefits	Other	Measures tracked specifically for people with disabilities
Navy Safe Harbor Program	•	•		•			•			•
Recovery Care Coordinator Program										
Recovery Coordination Program—Operation Warfighter				•	•		•			•
U.S. Special Operations Command Care Coalition			•	•						•
Department of Education										
American Indian Vocational Rehabilitation Services	•	•	•	•	•	•	•		•	•
Helen Keller National Center for Deaf-Blind Youths and Adults				•					•	•
Migrant and Seasonal Farmworkers				•		•				•

GAO-12-677 Employment for People with Disabilities

Program	Educational attainment	Credential attainment	Entered the military, postsecondary education, or vocational training program	Entered employment	Employment retention	Wage gain or change	Customer satisfaction	Reduced reliance on federal cash benefits	Other	Measures tracked specifically for people with disabilities
Model Comprehensive Transition and Postsecondary Programs for Students with Intellectual Disabilities		•								•
Randolph-Sheppard Vending Facilities Program				•		•				•
Rehabilitation Services Demonstration and Training Programs[a]	•	•	•	•		•			•	•
Assistive Technology State Grant program									•	•
Supported Employment State Grants				•		•		•	•	•
State Vocational Rehabilitation Services				•		•		•	•	•

	Educational attainment	Credential attainment	Entered the military, postsecondary education, or vocational training program	Entered employment	Employment retention	Wage gain or change	Customer satisfaction	Reduced reliance on federal cash benefits	Other	Measures tracked specifically for people with disabilities
Department of Health and Human Services										
1915(c) Home and Community Based Services Waiver										
1915(i) State Plan Home and Community-Based Services										
Medicaid State Plan Services										
Money Follows the Person Rebalancing Demonstration										
Department of Labor										
America's Heroes at Work										
Disabled Veterans' Outreach Program				●	●				●	●
Employer Assistance and Resource Network				●			●			●
Job Accommodation Network					●		●			●
Job Corps	●	●		●	●	●				●

	Educational attainment	Credential attainment	Entered the military, postsecondary education, or vocational training program	Entered employment	Employment retention	Wage gain or change	Customer satisfaction	Reduced reliance on federal cash benefits	Other	Measures tracked specifically for people with disabilities
Local Veterans' Employment Representatives program				●	●				●	●
REALifelines Initiative										●
Registered Apprenticeship for Youth and Young Adults with Disabilities Initiative	●	●	●	●	●				●	●
Community Service Employment for Older Americans/Senior Community Service Employment Program				●	●	●	●		●	●
Veterans' Workforce Investment Program				●	●				●	●
Work Opportunity Tax Credit (also under the Internal Revenue Service)			●	●		●			●	●
Workforce Investment Act Youth Activities	●	●	●	●	●				●	●

GAO-12-677 Employment for People with Disabilities

	Educational attainment	Credential attainment	Entered the military, postsecondary education, or vocational training program	Entered employment	Employment retention	Wage gain or change	Customer satisfaction	Reduced reliance on federal cash benefits	Other	Measures tracked specifically for people with disabilities
Workforce Recruitment Program (also under the Department of Defense)				•						•
YouthBuild	•	•	•	•	•	•			•	•
Department of Veterans Affairs										
Compensated Work Therapy program				•	•	•	•		•	•
Disabled Transition Assistance Program										
Vocational Rehabilitation and Employment			•	•	•	•			•	•
Vocational Training and Rehabilitation for Vietnam Veterans' Children with Spina Bifida or Other Covered Birth Defects										

	Educational attainment	Credential attainment	Entered the military, postsecondary education, or vocational training program	Entered employment	Employment retention	Wage gain or change	Customer satisfaction	Reduced reliance on federal cash benefits	Other	Measures tracked specifically for people with disabilities
Social Security Administration										
State Vocational Rehabilitation Cost Reimbursement Program				•	•			•		•
Ticket to Work program	•	•		•	•		•	•	•	•
Work Incentives Planning and Assistance program	•	•	•	•	•					•

Source: GAO survey.

[a] In commenting on a draft of this report, Education officials noted that Rehabilitation Services Demonstration and Training Programs may track some of these measures on a project-specific basis, depending on the purpose of the demonstration project.

Program (agency)	Impact study[a]	Other study
AgrAbility (Department of Agriculture)		•
Compensated Work Therapy program (Department of Veteran Affairs)		•
Employer Assistance and Resource Network (Labor)[b]		•
Helen Keller National Center (Education)		•
Job Corps (Labor)	•	
Mental Health Treatment Study (SSA)[c]	•	
Randolph Sheppard Vending Facilities Program (Education)[d]		•
Recovery Care Coordinator–Operation Warfighter (Department of Defense)		•
Ticket to Work program (SSA)		•
Work Incentives Planning and Assistance program (SSA)		•
Youth Transition Demonstration Projects (SSA)[c]	•	
YouthBuild (Labor)		•

Source: GAO survey.

[a]In response to our survey questions that asked whether any impact studies had been conducted, officials from five program provided references. We evaluated the methodology of each study and determined that three of them met the definition of an impact study provided in our questionnaire—a study that assessed the net effect of a program by comparing program outcomes with an estimate of what would have happened in the absence of the program—and had been completed since 2006. The other studies either did not meet our definition or were not available for review.

[b]This program reported having conducted an impact study, but that it was still in progress as part of a larger effort.

[c]Two of the three programs that conducted impact studies were excluded from our scope because they ended prior to April 2012, but are listed here because the studies are discussed in the report.

[d]This program cited a previous GAO study, which is not an program evaluation.

USDA

United States
Department of
Agriculture

Research,
Education, and
Economics

MAY 3 0 2012

National Institute
of Food and
Agriculture

1400 Independence
Avenue SW
Washington, DC
20250

TO: Daniel Bertoni, Director
         Education, Workforce and Income Security Issues, GAO

FROM: Edward Nwaba, Chief
         Oversight Branch
         Office of Grants and Financial Management

SUBJECT: Response to Draft Report GAO-12-677 Employment for People with
         Disabilities

Thank you for the opportunity to review and comment on Draft Report GAO-12-677.
The National Institute of Food and Agriculture generally concurs with the findings of the
report and has no additional comments to offer at this time.

Questions regarding this memorandum can be directed to Edward Nwaba, Oversight
Branch Chief and Agency Audit Liaison Official on (202) 205-5799 or via email at
enwaba@nifa.usda.gov.

USDA is an equal opportunity provider and employer

Appendix IX: Agency Comments from the Department of Education

UNITED STATES DEPARTMENT OF EDUCATION
OFFICE OF SPECIAL EDUCATION AND REHABILITATIVE SERVICES

THE ASSISTANT SECRETARY

JUN - 5 2012

Mr. Daniel Bertoni
Director
Education, Workforce and Income Security Issues
U.S. Government Accountability Office
441 G Street, NW
Washington, DC 20548

Dear Mr. Bertoni:

I am writing to provide the U.S. Government Accountability Office (GAO) with comments from the U.S. Department of Education (Department) on the draft report, "EMPLOYMENT FOR PEOPLE WITH DISABILITIES: Little is Known about the Effectiveness of Fragmented and Overlapping programs" (GAO-12-667).

While GAO has made no recommendations for executive action at this time, we were pleased at the draft report's observation that the Department's largest employment program, vocational rehabilitation (VR) state grants, is among those programs that more consistently coordinate with other key related programs at the federal level. We intend to continue to work with other Departments and agencies to improve continuously the effectiveness of the VR program, which is successful in providing employment outcomes for nearly 200,000 individuals annually, most of whom are identified as having significant or most significant disabilities.

The VR program achieves these employment results in part because state VR agencies coordinate services at the state and local service delivery level in several ways, which were not fully described in the draft report. At the state level, state VR agencies are mandatory partner programs within each state's workforce investment system. The system's One-Stop centers provide for coordination and cooperation at the service delivery level with programs funded under Title I of the Workforce Investment Act and other mandatory and optional One-Stop center partners. VR agencies have staff with specialized skills who provide a wide variety of education, training, and rehabilitation services to One-Stop customers with disabilities through individualized plans for employment.

The Rehabilitation Act of 1973, as amended, also requires state VR agencies to enter into agreements or other arrangements with state entities for the purpose of interagency coordination and service provision, including state Medicaid programs, American Indian VR services (AIVRS) programs in the state, state educational agencies, public institutions of higher education (IHEs), components of the workforce investment system (to coordinate services among agencies when individuals are served outside of the One-Stop centers), and any other appropriate public entities.

400 MARYLAND AVE. S.W., WASHINGTON, DC 20202-2500
www.ed.gov
The Department of Education's mission is to promote student achievement and preparation for global competitiveness by fostering educational excellence and ensuring equal access.

Mr. Daniel Bertoni – Page 2

Interagency agreements often exist between state VR agencies and other state and federal programs not specifically identified in statute. Examples include federal and state programs that serve veterans, state assistive technology programs, and state welfare agencies. In addition, a wide variety of similar agreements and arrangements exist at local levels, between state VR agencies and local public entity programs, individual IHEs, local school systems, Native American tribal service delivery programs, and many others.

The VR program emphasis on interagency coordination of service provision is also demonstrated in services to individual customers. State VR agencies seek out and coordinate the provision of services available from other programs for which an individual might be eligible (called comparable services and benefits), as part of the development of an individual's Individual Plan for Employment.

Taken together, the capacity of the Department's VR program to provide and coordinate a wide range of individualized services to achieve an employment outcome for individuals with disabilities, particularly significant disabilities, is not duplicated by any other program.

Likewise, our discretionary grant programs coordinate with other programs and services at the state and local levels in a variety of ways depending on the program. Coordination and collaboration is required in state plans and through requirements in grant applications, and informally. For example, the AIVRS programs must coordinate with state VR agencies to provide VR services to American Indians with disabilities living on or near reservations.

While the draft report provides some helpful information, it does not fully discuss the coordinated efforts that are taking place. Thank you for the opportunity to comment on this draft report. We have also forwarded technical comments and suggestions, which are enclosed. Please let me know if you have any questions about our comments.

Sincerely,

Alexa Posny

Alexa Posny, Ph.D.

Appendix X: Agency Comments from the Department of Labor

U.S. Department of Labor   Assistant Secretary for Policy
Washington, D.C. 20210

JUN 1 1 2012

Daniel Bertoni, Director
Education, Workforce, and Income Security Issues
U.S. Government Accountability Office
441 G Street N.W.
Washington, D.C. 20548

Dear Mr. Bertoni:

On behalf of the U.S. Department of Labor (Department), I want to thank you for the opportunity to review and comment on the Government Accountability Office's (GAO) draft language that will be included in GAO's Employment for People with Disabilities report (12-677). We are concerned about the GAO's general statement that finds fragmentation within the programs it examined. We respectfully recommend that the GAO reconsider and refine its findings to better reflect the information in this letter.

In the report, the GAO notes that over the years many programs have been created to address issues related to the employment of people with disabilities. However, several of the Department's programs included in the study were not created solely for this purpose, but rather to provide services to all job seekers -- the majority of whom are not individuals with disabilities. This report suggests that because they are available to any youth with disabilities, certain programs present a greater risk of duplication than segregated disability programs that focus on a single specific subpopulation of people with disabilities. In so concluding, the GAO fails to recognize that the actual services provided, program design used, and the populations served in the Department's programs vary considerably. Moreover, the Labor Department is proud that we have made great strides in accessibility, and that employment and training programs administered by the Department serve people with disabilities alongside their peers. Rather than being duplicative or undesirable, we believe that service integration and diversity of design are important for achieving inclusion of people with disabilities consistent with disability civil rights laws enacted by Congress.

The Department is committed to working with its Federal agency partners on a variety of efforts to better respond to both current and future workforce needs, and to leverage resources to help individuals, including those with disabilities, find and keep good jobs. While we agree that it is important to minimize duplication and maximize efficiency, the Department wants to emphasize that some overlap between programs is necessary and appropriate to ensure that all participants receive comprehensive employment and training services. We believe that a coherent public workforce system does not necessarily mean a single program, supplier, or agency. Our goal is a rational system with pieces that fit together logically, with minimal duplication. This system can provide ready and seamless access to services for both jobseekers – including individuals with disabilities – and employers looking for job-ready skilled workers.

If you would like additional information, please do not hesitate to call me at 202-693-5959. The Department is also available and willing to meet with GAO to discuss this letter. The Department appreciates the work being done by GAO to improve efficiency in government. We also believe great progress has been made over the years within the Labor Department. As our nation rises to meet the current fiscal challenges, please be assured that we will continue to work closely with GAO to maximize our nation's resources.

Sincerely,

William E. Spriggs
Assistant Secretary for Policy

Appendix XI: GAO Contact and Staff Acknowledgments

GAO Contact	Daniel Bertoni, (202) 512-7215 or bertonid@gao.gov
Staff Acknowledgments	Michele Grgich, Assistant Director; Rachael Chamberlin Valliere, Analyst-in-Charge; Margaret J. Weber; and Miriam Hill made significant contributions to all aspects of this engagement. Stuart M. Kaufmann, Christine C. San, and Walter Vance assisted with the methodology, survey development, and data analysis. Jessica A. Botsford and Sheila McCoy provided legal assistance. Kate van Gelder and James Bennett helped prepare the final report and graphics. Tom Moscovitch, John S. Townes, and Jacques Arsenault verified our findings.

GAO's Mission	The Government Accountability Office, the audit, evaluation, and investigative arm of Congress, exists to support Congress in meeting its constitutional responsibilities and to help improve the performance and accountability of the federal government for the American people. GAO examines the use of public funds; evaluates federal programs and policies; and provides analyses, recommendations, and other assistance to help Congress make informed oversight, policy, and funding decisions. GAO's commitment to good government is reflected in its core values of accountability, integrity, and reliability.
Obtaining Copies of GAO Reports and Testimony	The fastest and easiest way to obtain copies of GAO documents at no cost is through GAO's website (www.gao.gov). Each weekday afternoon, GAO posts on its website newly released reports, testimony, and correspondence. To have GAO e-mail you a list of newly posted products, go to www.gao.gov and select "E-mail Updates."
Order by Phone	The price of each GAO publication reflects GAO's actual cost of production and distribution and depends on the number of pages in the publication and whether the publication is printed in color or black and white. Pricing and ordering information is posted on GAO's website, http://www.gao.gov/ordering.htm. Place orders by calling (202) 512-6000, toll free (866) 801-7077, or TDD (202) 512-2537. Orders may be paid for using American Express, Discover Card, MasterCard, Visa, check, or money order. Call for additional information.
Connect with GAO	Connect with GAO on Facebook, Flickr, Twitter, and YouTube. Subscribe to our RSS Feeds or E-mail Updates. Listen to our Podcasts. Visit GAO on the web at www.gao.gov.
To Report Fraud, Waste, and Abuse in Federal Programs	Contact: Website: www.gao.gov/fraudnet/fraudnet.htm E-mail: fraudnet@gao.gov Automated answering system: (800) 424-5454 or (202) 512-7470
Congressional Relations	Katherine Siggerud, Managing Director, siggerudk@gao.gov, (202) 512-4400, U.S. Government Accountability Office, 441 G Street NW, Room 7125, Washington, DC 20548
Public Affairs	Chuck Young, Managing Director, youngc1@gao.gov, (202) 512-4800 U.S. Government Accountability Office, 441 G Street NW, Room 7149 Washington, DC 20548

Please Print on Recycled Paper.